"Information through Innovation"

HANDS-ON INTERNET
for Windows

Neil J. Salkind
University of Kansas

bf

boyd & fraser publishing company

I(T)P An International Thomson Publishing Company

Danvers • Albany • Bonn • Boston • Cincinnati • Detroit • London • Madrid • Melbourne
Mexico City • New York • Paris • San Francisco • Singapore • Tokyo • Toronto • Washington

To my best friend, with love and affection

Publishing Process Director: Carol Crowell
Acquisitions Editor: Rita Ferrandino
Production Editor: Jean Bermingham
Composition: Rebecca Evans & Associates
Interior Design: Rebecca Evans & Associates
Cover Design: Kevin Meyers
Manufacturing Coordinator: Lisa Flanagan
Marketing Director: William Lisowski

I(T)P The ITP™ logo is a trademark under license.

Printed in the United States of America

For more information, contact boyd & fraser publishing company:

boyd & fraser publishing company
One Corporate Place • Ferncroft Village
Danvers, Massachusetts 01923, USA

International Thomson Editores
Campose Eliseos 385, Piso 7
Col. Polanco
11560 Mexico D.F. Mexico

International Thomson Publishing Europe
Berkshire House 168-173
High Holborn
London, WC1V 7AA, England

International Thomson Publishing GmbH
Konigswinterer Strasse 418
53227 Bonn, Germany

Thomas Nelson Australia
102 Dodds Street
South Melbourne 3205
Victoria, Australia

International Thomson Publishing Asia
221 Henderson Road
#05-10 Henderson Building
Singapore 0315

Nelson Canada
1120 Birchmount Road
Scarborough, Ontario
Canada M1K 5G4

International Thomson Publishing Japan
Hirakawacho Kyowa Building, 3F
2-2-1 Hirakawacho
Chiyoda-ku, Tokyo 102, Japan

1 2 3 4 5 6 7 8 9 10 BN 9 8 7 6 5

ISBN: 0-7895-0170-8

Contents

Preface

Everyday, we're deluged with information about everything from the score of last night's football game to the latest food scare to Congressional committee business to the weather reports. While the information has always been there, the information superhighway has not. Today, all it takes is a personal computer and some connection software to make anyone an information equal of anyone else. And now, with Windows-based tools available for accessing this information, things look more attractive then ever.

That's where the Internet and *Hands-On Internet for Windows* comes in. My goal in writing this book is to give you a hands-on overview of what type of information is available on the Internet and how you can access it. I tried to stay away from technical talk and get straight to the procedures you will find most valuable. Tech talk is important if you want to go beyond just using the Internet and understand the dynamics of telecommunications. But for now, we'll just concentrate on the basics.

ORGANIZATION OF THE BOOK

Hands-On Internet for Windows is organized into eight chapters.

Chapter 1 describes the Internet, how and when it developed, some of the things you can do on the Net, and some general guidelines for behavior when using the Internet.

Chapter 2 explains how to connect to the Internet, the different types of Internet connections, how people and places are named on the Net, and the importance of passwords.

Chapter 3 focuses on how to browse the Net and the World Wide Web (also known as WWW or W^3). Home pages, dynamic links, URL's and http will become your second language, and you'll have more fun than you would have imagined.

For many people, e-mail is the only reason they use the Internet. Chapter 4 shows you how to use Netscape to send mail and introduces the fully-featured mail program Eudora (named after the author Eudora Welty).

Chapter 5 begins our journey into what's available on the Internet. Using file transfer protocol, you can go to one of thousands of computers and discover the millions of files that exist on everything from NASA photos to games. Then, with a few simple commands, you can transfer these files to your computer and explore them at your leisure.

All the News That's Fit to Print might be the New York Times' banner, but newsgroups (Chapter 6) are where all the news you might want to read is at. From more than 30,000 newsgroups, you can select the articles you want to read about everything from archery to automobiles, and you can contribute your own observations as well. These on-line bulletin boards allow you to learn and exchange ideas and views.

Chapter 7 introduces you to the telnet command, which you can use to go to another computer such as the online catalog at the Library of Congress, and remotely access information.

Finally, Chapter 8 provides an overview of Internet utilities and how they are used. These utilities, such as Archie and Veronica, help you search through thousands of Internet locations to find a file or some information. The Internet utility Gopher allows you to go from Internet site to Internet site with the press of a key to track down important information.

Appendix A contains a list of resources on the Internet. Appendix B contains hints on how to get out of trouble once you're in it (which happens to all of us once in a while!). Appendix C contains the answers to the end-of-chapter Review Questions and Exploration Exercises. Appendix D discusses the changing nature of Netscape.

OUTSTANDING FEATURES OF THE BOOK

Readability. Any book, especially one that deals with such technical material as the Internet, must communicate ideas and transmit information. This book is carefully organized with logical presentation of topics. The information is presented at a level that is understandable for the beginning student.

Advance Organizers. Each chapter begins with a brief list of what the student will be expected to have mastered after the chapter and the chapter exercises are completed.

Key Words. At the end of each chapter is a list of the important terms that were introduced in that chapter. Each term first appears in bold in the chapter.

How To Boxes. Throughout *Hands-On Internet for Windows*, step-by-step instructions on how to perform certain tasks are integrated into the chapter material and physically set off so the student can see immediately what steps are necessary to perform such tasks.

Illustrations. Hands-On Internet for Windows contains many illustrations showing how to perform important tasks. Students are encouraged to participate in these hands-on exercises. The accompanying screens show what they can expect to see as a result of their efforts.

Exercises. Each chapter ends with two types of exercises. The first, Review Questions, are a set of substantive questions about the content of the chapter. The second type, Exploration Exercises, are hands-on exercises that take the student into the Internet and provide an opportunity to practice Internet skills. Answers to these exercises are contained in Appendix C.

For the instructor, a printed test bank (available on disk as well) is available.

HOW TO USE HANDS-ON INTERNET FOR WINDOWS

Before you get started, just a few notes about the conventions used in this book.

1. When you are supposed to type or click something, it will appear in color in the step, such as

   Click File.

2. When you see press Enter, it means to press the Enter (or Return) key.

3. IMPORTANT! IMPORTANT! IMPORTANT! Throughout *Hands-On Internet for Windows* there are many illustrations of what the Internet looks like. But, since the Internet is changing everyday, what you see on your screen may not be exactly the same as what you see in the book. The differences should be small and relatively insignificant. Don't panic. You should have no problem understanding what's on your screen and how it relates to the material in the book.

A SPECIAL NOTE TO STUDENTS

Learning any new endeavor is not easy, but it's always worth it. Here are some Do's and Dont's that will help you as you work through *Hands-On Internet for Windows*.

Some Do's

- *Do* browse through the entire book to get some idea about what material is covered and in what order it is presented. Everything covered is important for you to learn.

- *Do* browse at your leisure, and don't worry about reading each chapter in detail, taking notes, or memorizing the meaning of terms or important keystrokes. As you work through the individual chapters, you will get a chance to concentrate on detail.

- *Do* read through each chapter before you begin working on your computer. Try to visualize what might happen on the screen as the activity is described in the book. Also, read through the examples and exercises so you can get some idea of what you will be expected to do when you begin your "hands on" training.

- *Do* follow the directions in each section closely, and do exactly what the instruction asks you to do.

- *Do* try the examples as they are presented in the text.

- *Do* keep trying to get the example correct before you move on. While every effort was made to make the examples "fail proof," you might find yourself confused and not comfortable with the material. If this happens, go back to the beginning of the chapter and start over.

- *Do* the exercises at the end of each chapter and check your answers with a classmate. You might also want to form a study group to review material and practice using the Internet. This way you can check your work and help each other generate new ideas about the Net.

Some Don'ts

- *Don't* fall behind. It is very difficult to catch up. You don't need the extra pressure along with your other classes and work. By the way, this is good advice for any class.

- *Don't* study or work for too long a time when you first begin to learn about the Internet. You will end up tired and frustrated. Instead, work in small chunks of time, giving yourself ample time between work sessions. You know your own pace. One suggestion is to cover no more than a chapter a day, including exercises.

- *Don't* jump around. Each part of *Hands-On Internet for Windows* is organized in a sequence of chapters that will get you started using the Net. Try to follow the chapters in the sequence presented.

- Finally, be adventurous and explore the Net every chance you get. As you will learn, the Internet is full of treasures waiting to be found. You may have to do some digging, but along the way you are certain to find interesting, useful, and fun things that make the trip worth while.

ACKNOWLEDGMENTS

I have many people to thank for their suggestions, guidance, and encouragement: Rita Ferrandino, Acquisitions Editor, for offering me the opportunity to write the book; Jean Bermingham, Production Editor, for handling production; and Joan Paterson, for a great copyediting job. Thanks also to the following reviewers:

Tim Gottleber, Northlake College

David John Jankowski, California State University at San Marcos

Dixie Lynn Massaro, Irvine Valley College

Special thanks go to Terry, Jill, Larry, Victor, Wes, Kim, Judy, Laura, Brian, Josh, Kandace, and Singh.

Neil J. Salkind

1

Say Hello to the Internet

After completing this chapter, you'll be able to

- Define the Internet
- Explain how the Internet started
- Understand why the demand for the Internet is growing at a phenomenal rate
- Understand how the Internet operates
- Understand the various ways you can use the Internet
- Explain why Internet etiquette is important
- Understand the rules of the Internet

Last night I sat down at my computer, learned a great new joke from this giant collection of jokes, wrote to President Bill Clinton about health care, talked to my friend Lew in North Carolina, found a synonym by consulting *Roget's Thesaurus*, and read about making my own beer in the *Homebrew Digest*. I was going to read a chapter of *Moby Dick*, but decided it was too late.

I did this all from my computer by accessing the Internet, the international highway system of the electronic age. The Internet is like the New Jersey Turnpike: it can be challenging to get on and navigate, but once you are there, there are literally thousands of places you can go.

WHAT IS THE INTERNET? In the most basic terms, the **Internet** (commonly referred to as the **Net**) is a **network** of networks. What's a network? It is a collection of computers that are connected to one another and can communicate with each other. For example, at your college or university, the members of the psychology department may be on a network where electronic mail (e-mail) can be sent and received from office to office. The English, Spanish, and art departments may have networks of their own as well.

Imagine if all these networks were connected to one another, like you see in Figure 1.1. This is an example of how only a few networks can be connected. Now imagine hundreds of networks and thousands of computers of all different types connected to one another and millions of people using those computers—that's the Internet. The Internet's an amazing tool and throughout *Hands-On Internet for Windows* we'll tell you why and show you how to use it.

FIGURE 1.1
Networks connected to networks. Welcome to the Internet.

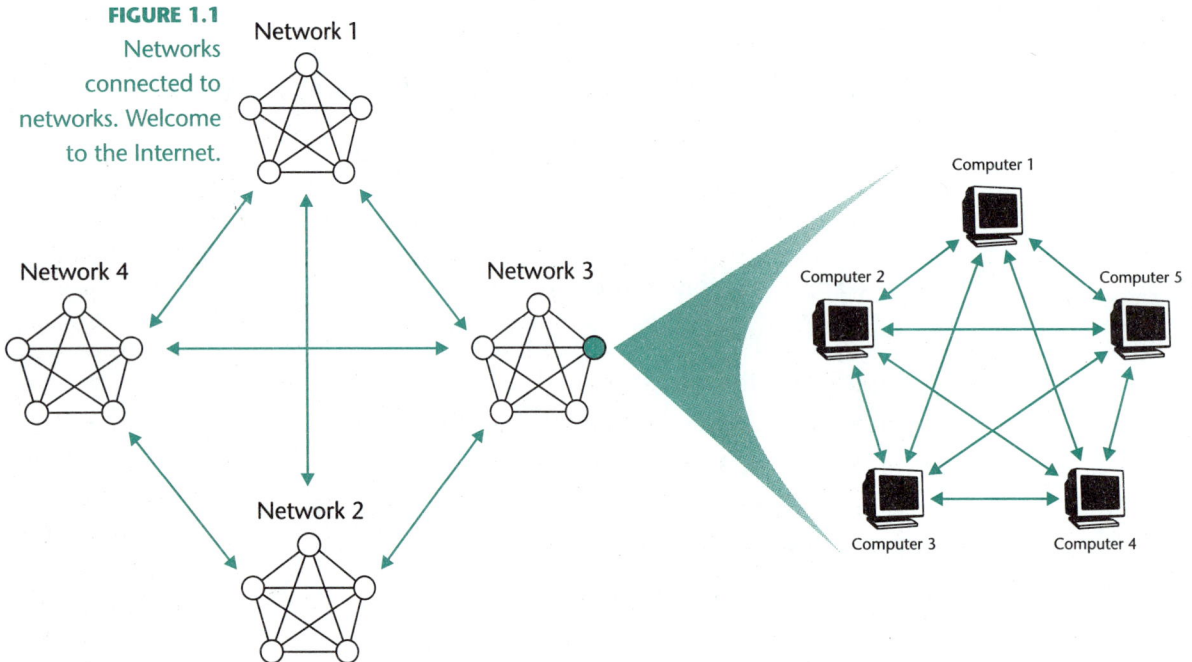

HISTORY OF THE INTERNET

In 1969, the Department of Defense developed a way to network or connect military contractors who were working on grants from the department. This initial network was called **ARPANET** (for *Advanced Research Projects Agency NET*). It is like a grandparent to the Internet.

Things went very well with ARPANET and before long, everyone (universities, private research labs, and individuals) wanted to be connected. While it was not entirely clear what the potential was, many people realized that being able to communicate electronically was the first step in the future growth of technology dealing with the flow of information.

ARPANET was so successful and grew so quickly that another network was needed to handle all the traffic. Hence, a new network named **MILNET** (*Military Net*) was created in 1983. Although these were two independent networks, much of the work that went on within one was related to work going on within the other. It only made sense to develop a technique for sharing information between them. Once again, necessity was the mother of invention, and a technique for allowing network traffic to be routed from one network to another was developed. This tool came to be called the **Internet Protocol** or the **IP** (a protocol is a way of doing things). The business of the Internet Protocol was to make sure that information was not garbled as it was transmitted between **sites**, that is, the locations where Internet connections are made.

As you might imagine, once word got out that information could be quickly shared across thousands of miles with relative ease, many organizations and individuals wanted access to the information highway. With computers being so accessible and on-line connections only a phone call away, networks began to grow.

One of the first big networks, funded by IBM to connect universities and research labs, was **BITNET**, which stands for *Because It's Time* (some network humor there). Developed at the City University of New York as an electronic mail (e-mail) tool, it quickly found a home at most major colleges and universities. Since then, almost every school is on BITNET and other networks as well.

The U.S. government, in the form of the National Science Foundation, eventually realized the potential of what the electronic transmission of information could mean, and in 1986 dedicated five huge supercomputers to providing computing power to universities and research institutions. Before this time, these supercomputers were mostly used to design weapons. While large companies used them to model the weather and do geological research, these computers were not accessible to the average U.S. citizen.

With these new, more powerful machines available and on-line, e-mail and other documents were more easily and more efficiently sent from site to site. More sites became available and the growth of the Net really began to take off. The **NSFNET** (*National Science Foundation NET*) linked thousands of computers and worked so well that the ARPANET was retired. How well did NSFNET work? Take a look at the graph in Figure 1.2 and see how in a bit more than 20 years, the descendants of ARPANET have grown from a handful of connections on a network to more than 2 million! And today, between 1,000 and 1,500 **hosts** (another term for Internet sites) are being added *every month*. The number of individuals connected to these sites is more than 30 million and growing every day. While nobody really knows how many people use the Internet, almost everyone knows that the Internet is an uncharted and very popular place to explore. By the way, the numbers for this chart came from the ultimate time line of the history of the Internet compiled and maintained by Robert H'obbes' Zakon. You can find out how to get the entire time line in Appendix A.

The increased demand for on-line communication has occurred for several reasons. First, information has become an important and valuable commodity. Companies, governments, research organizations, and private individuals recognize that having the necessary information about a particular topic, issue, or product can mean success. Information increases one's competitive advantage whether you are trying to find patents for a waterproof gizmo or the latest census numbers.

Secondly, where the Net was once the province of big organizations, individual users are now being solicited to join through commercial Internet services

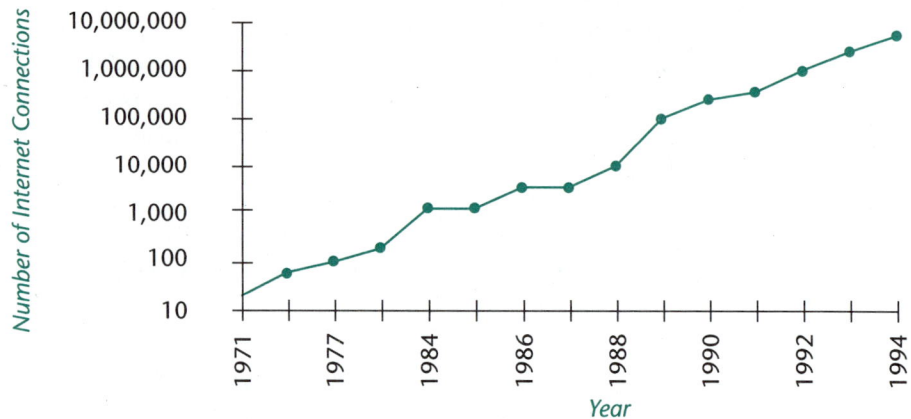

such as Delphi, CompuServe, and America OnLine. Commercial Internet services provide a connection to the Internet for a fee. We'll talk more about these services in Chapter 2.

Finally, and perhaps best of all, the Internet is so much fun, so addictive, and so instructive that you'll find yourself experiencing what M. Csikszentmihalyi, a University of Chicago psychologist, calls **flow**. Flow occurs when you become so involved in what you are doing that you lose track of time. You sign on, check your mail, play a game, read a bit of a novel, go to another computer to find a long-lost friend's e-mail address, and on and on. You look up to check the clock. It's 4A.M. and you wonder how time can go by so fast.

HOW THE INTERNET OPERATES

Today, the Internet is not run by any one organization or individual. It's not a company; there are no direct monthly charges or dues. Almost anyone can use it and there's no boss! So who's in charge?

Remember, the Internet is a network of networks. Each network has a manager or a **system administrator** who is responsible for making sure that things run smoothly and that everyone acts appropriately while they are using the network. While the Internet is not as highly structured as a large corporation or business, there are groups that help manage the Internet (see Figure 1.3). The one group that seems to have the most influence is the **Internet Society** or **ISOC**, formed in January 1992 to promote the exchange of information through the Internet and the advancement of Internet technology.

Some of the ISOC's primary goals are to

- Encourage use of the Net by research organizations, businesses, and the public
- Explore standards for use of the Internet including the transmission of information from site to site, management of the Internet, and access to the Internet
- Investigate new uses of the Internet

FIGURE 1.3

How the Internet
is governed.

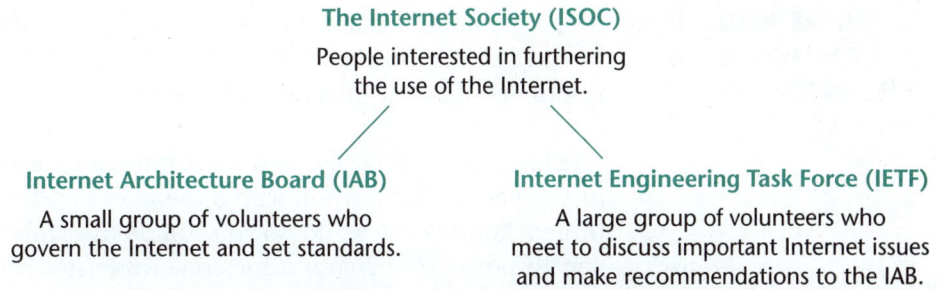

The Internet Society (ISOC)

People interested in furthering
the use of the Internet.

Internet Architecture Board (IAB)

A small group of volunteers who
govern the Internet and set standards.

Internet Engineering Task Force (IETF)

A large group of volunteers who
meet to discuss important Internet issues
and make recommendations to the IAB.

Part of the ISOC is a group of experienced volunteers who are invited (by the membership) to become part of the **Internet Architecture Board** or **IAB.** These Internet gurus help set policy, institute standards, and discuss issues such as the role of censorship in the sharing of information electronically. These are the people who, for example, set the rules and standards for assigning electronic mail addresses, so no two people have the same address.

There's another Internet group that plays an important role in the way the Internet continues to evolve: the **Internet Engineering Task Force,** or **IETF.** This group of volunteers focuses on short-term technical problems such as the adoption of standard software or how new Internet sites will be named. Once the IETF finishes their work, their report is disseminated (electronically, of course) to ISOC members and sent on to the IAB. The IAB then decides whether to accept the suggested changes as Internet standards.

If you have any interest in helping govern the Internet, you can participate at various levels. You can talk to your instructor or your system administrator about learning more about the structure of the Internet at your own college or university. It would be fun and useful to observe the activities of the person in charge of the Internet's operation at your site. Your college or university might even have a local governance board right on campus which may welcome a student member. If you want to become involved beyond the local level, contact and join the Internet Society. Its address is 12020 Sunrise Valley Drive, Suite 270, Reston, VA 22091. Their phone number is (703) 648–9888, and their electronic mail address is isoc@isoc.org. In Chapter 4, you'll learn how to write to the Society electronically.

On the campus level, the system administrator is in charge of seeing that Internet business is attended to. This is the person who assigns Internet addresses, manages the network, makes sure that Internet traffic gets sent on to the next network, moderates the type and use of Internet news, and sets local standards such as which kind of software will be used to access the Internet, as well as many other tasks.

The cost for all this is paid by the individual networks that make up the Internet. For example, the cost of running NSFNET is paid by the National Science Foundation. The cost of maintaining the network and its Internet connection at your local college or university is paid by student fees and other revenues your school collects. All the individual networks on the Internet pay their own way.

If you're talking about information in all shapes and sizes, there's not much that you can't do on the Net. Here's a brief overview of how the Net is used. We'll go into detail about each one later on in *Hands-On Internet for Windows.*

- The Internet is probably used most often for electronic mail or e-mail. Just as you exchange mail with a friend or business associate across the United States or the world, so you can do the same without ever placing pen to paper. You create a message and send it to your destination's electronic address. It's fast, easy, and fun.

  For example, recently I attended my thirtieth high school reunion. When I got home, there was an e-mail message from a woman who was a class-mate in high school. I had asked her for the e-mail address of someone I was wondering about who couldn't attend the reunion. You'll learn about sending and receiving e-mail in Chapter 4.

- Information, information, information—all available in millions of files on the Net. Using **file transfer protocol** (**ftp)**, you can **download** or transfer files from other locations to your computer. With a little prac-tice, you can "surf" the Net for recipes, screen savers for your DOS- or Mac-based machine, holdings of the University of Kansas history collec-tion, and the lyrics to sixties' rock-and-roll hits.

  For example, it was time to cook dinner and neither Bob nor Carol had any idea what to make. Bob turned to the Net, found an easy recipe for spaghetti carbonara, downloaded the recipe, and had the dish on the table (much to Carol's approval) in 20 minutes. You'll learn all about ftp and accessing files in Chapter 5.

- There are thousands of electronic newsgroups available to you on the Internet. These are places where information on topics ranging from space exploration to the authenticity of a Civil War era land deed can be posted and shared among Internet users. You can drop in and con-tribute to any of these newsgroups.

  For example, Bob Dylan was in Lawrence, Kansas, for a concert in April 1994. The tickets went on sale at 8 A.M. two months before the concert date, but the line had already started forming by 6 A.M.. About two weeks before the concert, the alt.music.dylan newsgroup section had the mes-sage, "Anyone with Dylan tickets for the Lawrence concert, I'll pay pre-mium prices!" In Chapter 6 you will learn how to discover the latest on the soap operas or investigate what kind of car you should consider buying by consulting with the appropriate newsgroup.

- When you **telnet**, or connect to a remote site, it's as if you were using a computer at another location. With an Internet connection, you can control computers thousands of miles away and get the information that these computers have access to. You can have some outrageous fun as well, such as finding out how many bottles of cold Sprite are in the Coke machine in the Computer Science building at MIT!

For example, wanting to know what other works a particular author had completed, I telneted to the Library of Congress and entered the author's full name. In a second, there was a list of his forty other titles. You'll learn how to do this in Chapter 7.

- Finger, WHOIS, Archie, Veronica, and the World Wide Web are Internet utilities that help you search for and find information, such as the location of a certain software program you want to use or the e-mail address of a friend.

For example, Jack was just getting started using e-mail but did not know his son's e-mail address. A good friend used the Finger and the WHOIS commands to find the son's address. Jack was on-line with his son that same day. In Chapter 8, "Using Internet Utilities," you'll learn how to use these tools.

THE TEN INTERNET COMMANDMENTS

Although these commandments didn't come down from a mountain on stone tablets, they're good advice. Read them and try to adhere to them.

Commandment 1: Be Sure You're Connected

For beginners, it is not always clear whether or not you are actually connected to the Internet even when you think you may be. Use a host near to you to confirm you are up and running. How do you know? Most hosts send you back some kind of message indicating that you are connected. If you really can't find out if you're connected, turn to Appendix B on "Getting Out of Trouble."

Commandment 2: Once You Press the Key, It's Over

There's no recalling keystrokes. Once you press Enter or execute a command such as send mail, it's done. This is especially important when it comes to e-mail. Once you send that angry letter, there's no going to the mailbox and fishing it out. You need to be extra careful and extra sure of what you say and what you want to do before you do it electronically.

Commandment 3: Typing Counts and Sometimes Case Does as Well

One of the idiosyncracies of some operating systems on the Internet and the computers connected to it is that uppercase (such as A, B, C) and lowercase (such as a, b, c) have different meanings. Many Internet connections require you to use uppercase to sign on. If your password is *Sara*, then *sara* may not work. Also, type carefully. The Internet often demands long names and addresses. It's easy to type njs@falcon.cc.ukans.**eud** rather than njs@ukans.cc.**edu** and spend the next hour trying to figure out why you couldn't connect. New Internet users (often called newbies) spend a lot of time trying to figure out why their Internet connection doesn't work. Often the problem is that they have incorrectly typed the address where they want to send their message.

Commandment 4: Be Flexible About When and How You Use the Internet

Internet connections may be very busy places, especially if you try to locate or download a file during regular business hours (8A.M. to 5P.M.). If you choose to work during these hours, you will have to be patient, since it will take longer to do almost everything. Better yet, work on your Internet e-mail and other Internet activities after dinner, during the late evening hours, or even on the weekend. Usage is much less at these times because institutional, research, and business users are not on-line.

Commandment 5: Not All Internet Sites Are Created Equal

The Internet site you are connected to may not offer the same features as another. For example, your Internet connection may not have software for easily sending mail such as Eudora or web browsers such as Mosaic, Netscape, or Cello. Or, it may not have access to all the newsgroups you are interested in. If you have a choice, try to find out which services different Internet providers make available before you make a commitment to sign up.

Commandment 6: There's More Stuff Out There Than Anyone Can Know About

When you get on the Internet for the first time, you probably will not be able to contain your enthusiasm for what's ahead of you. That's great, but don't get carried away. There are thousands and thousands—maybe even millions—of files and resources out there on the Net for you to access and use. It will take you months to discover everything, and even then there will be more because the Net is growing every day. Take a little bit at a time and be successful rather than surfing all over the Net and getting frustrated. You might want to keep a pencil and paper handy to record your travels and stops along the way.

Commandment 7: Be Considerate of Others and Play by the Rules

You already know that there is no central Internet authority that controls every network on the Internet. Unless there were some rules or etiquette to follow, it's likely that the Internet would self-destruct, as would any large organization that had no guidelines. For that reason a set of informal and unenforced rules has evolved. These rules are called **netiquette**. We'll discuss the general rules later in this chapter and the specific ones later in the book.

Commandment 8: Practice, Practice, Practice

The more you practice, the more you will learn and the more useful the Internet will be to you. When you first get started, however, take your time and limit your efforts to an hour or less. This will prevent you from becoming fatigued and frustrated. An extra benefit of practicing is finding new Internet resources (such as new newsgroups or new programs) and undocumented Internet shortcuts.

Commandment 9: Be Patient with Yourself

Learning to use the Internet is not like learning to use a new word processor or play a new game. There is little documentation and no one program to run everything. If you have difficulty at first, don't quit. Follow the examples in this book, read as much as you can about the Internet, attend other classes if they are offered at your college, talk to others, and you will find yourself successful. Above all, explore—and don't take anything too seriously.

Commandment 10: Ask Others for Help and Help Others

A tremendous amount of valuable information comes from other users rather than from documentation such as user manuals, write-ups, and technical papers. You can learn a significant amount by reading the documentation for an application or a system (and even by reading some books as well!). You can also learn many other important tips, tricks, and clues from that person sitting next to you in the computer lab or a good friend who's been around the block a few more times than you. Ask politely for help and pay back that debt by helping others when you learn new and interesting things.

NETIQUETTE: HOW TO BE NICE ON THE NET

Commandment 7 stresses the importance of being considerate of others and playing by the rules. Where do these rules come from and what are they? For the most part, these rules have evolved out of the need for order on the Net. For example, many organizations follow *Robert's Rules of Order*, which dates back to 1876 and is based on British parliamentary law. *Robert's Rules* provides a set of guidelines for running a meeting. It spells out very clearly such practices as who leads the meeting, how a meeting should be run, who can speak when, how votes should be taken, and so on. If there are only four people at a meeting, then such rules are usually unnecessary because everything can be managed through consensus. However, when there are 30 million participants, some set of operating standards needs to be articulated and followed.

　　Robert's Rules is not applicable to the Internet, but another set is. That's the set of guidelines referred to as **netiquette**, a set of commonly accepted rules for using the Internet that has evolved over the years. These were developed because early Internet users realized that some set of rules for on-line behavior had to be established for the business of the Internet to get done. For example, if vulgarity was not frowned upon, it would be uncomfortable and uninviting for many Internet users to participate. These rules and guidelines have been suggested by everyday Internet users like you and me and are considered good for the Internet. They don't unreasonably restrict anyone's behavior. They just make it easier for everyone to carry out their own Internet business.

What follows are some of the general netiquette rules. It's up to the Internet membership (users like you and me) to adhere to this communal set of rules. As you work through *Hands-On Internet for Windows*, you will see Netiquette Boxes that talk about more specific rules for Internet activities such as mail and newsgroups.

- Above all, behavior on the Internet is the responsibility of the individual. You own your own words, so say what you mean and mean what you say. This is especially true with e-mail and newsgroup contributions.

- Individual differences are to be fostered and respected. You might disagree with someone's opinion about a book, her view of a raging philosophical debate, or her political viewpoint, but the free exchange of information, and not the censorship of that information, is one of the primary goals of the Internet.

- Don't intimidate, insult, or verbally abuse anyone. The same good manners you use in your home and everyday interactions should be used on the Internet.

- What's yours is yours and what's not is not. Be sure you don't unintentionally appropriate other people's materials as your own. In other words, taking something from the Internet that someone else wrote and claiming it's your own is as bad as copying someone else's term paper and submitting it as your own.

- The key to the success of the Internet is self-regulation. Even at 3A.M., you are still using resources. So if you want play Kung-Wung-Fu for five straight hours, don't. Play for an hour and give other people wanting to use the system a break. This is especially true if you are accessing the Internet through a phone line connection where there is a limited number of phone lines.

- Avoid sending junk mail. In Chapter 3, you'll see how you can send the same message to many people all at once. Announcing a meeting to your staff is quite different from sending a chain letter or a commercial message. Junk mail ties up valuable resources and it's not an appropriate use of the Internet.

- **Flaming** is being nasty in words or spirit—don't be!

- If you do need to download a substantial number of files, do it during off-business hours (generally 6P.M. to 8A.M.), when traffic is a bit slower. But remember, the Internet is a global community. What might be 10P.M. in your warm house on Main Street in Lawrence, Kansas, is 5P.M. in London.

As you work through *Hands-On Internet for Windows*, we'll introduce you to the particular guidelines for using the Net. In each chapter, you'll find helpful hints about how to remain a good Net citizen.

You probably know more now about the Internet than when you started reading Hands-On Internet for Windows, but not nearly as much as you will know when you are finished. The Internet has as much potential as a source of information for you as your willingness to investigate the Net will allow. The more you use it, the more you will learn and the more you will find the Internet to be an indispensable tool for your academic, professional, and personal work.

KEY WORDS

ARPANET	Internet Protocol (IP)
download	Internet Society (ISOC)
file transfer protocol (ftp)	MILNET
BITNET	Net
flaming	netiquette
flow	network
hosts	NSFNET
Internet	sites
Internet Architecture Board (IAB)	system admistrator
Internet Engineering Task Force (IETF)	telnet

REVIEW QUESTIONS

1. What role has the government played, and continues to play, in the development and maintenance of the Internet?

2. How is the Internet managed? Who pays for it? How can we all assure that it continues to be the valuable service it is?

3. Provide three different examples of how etiquette on the Internet would be violated. Why do the rules of Internet usage need to be adhered to?

4. How do you envision using the Internet? Try to gaze a bit into the future and speculate how the Internet might be used at your school. How might it be used in your everyday life in ten years?

5. Ask a faculty member at your college or university, a colleague in another department, or anyone you know who uses the Internet the following questions.
   - How did you learn about the Internet?

   - What do you mostly use the Internet for?

   - What advice would you give a new Internet user?

EXPLORATION EXERCISES

1. Write down three general information questions that you might want answered using the Internet's vast resources. For example,

   - Which professional baseball player had the highest lifetime batting average?

   - In what year was Richard Nixon born?

   - How do I make hummus?

   Later on, you will learn how to get answers for questions like these.

2. Go to the library and find five articles on the Internet. Look in the *Reader's Guide to Periodical Literature* for a start. Summarize these and point out what information the articles have in common with another student's responses. What is the coolest, most interesting, or fun thing you found out about the Internet?

Connecting to the Internet

After completing this chapter, you'll be able to

- Identify hardware and software needed to connect to the Internet
- Explain the difference between a dedicated connection and a dial-up connection
- Select a commercial Internet provider to connect to the Internet
- Identify what hardware and software components you need to access the Internet
- Understand how the Internet assigns and uses names and addresses
- Create and use a password

You know something about the Internet, for example, how it got started, how quickly it's growing, and what some of the things are that you can do on the Net. What you don't know yet and are about to learn is how to connect to the Internet. That's the first step in learning how to use the Internet. So let's get started.

ACCESSING THE INTERNET

There are two types of Internet connections: a dedicated connection and a dial-up connection. As you can see in Figure 2.1, a dedicated connection is the most direct of the two while a dial-up connection goes through phone lines first. We'll talk about the details of both types of connections now.

Dedicated Connections

A **dedicated connection** provides a direct line right into the Internet. There is no waiting for the phone line to be free or for the connection to be open. It's always open and always accessible. Therefore, dedicated connections to the Internet are the fastest but also the most expensive. A dedicated connection

13

FIGURE 2.1

A dedicated and dial-up connection to the Internet.

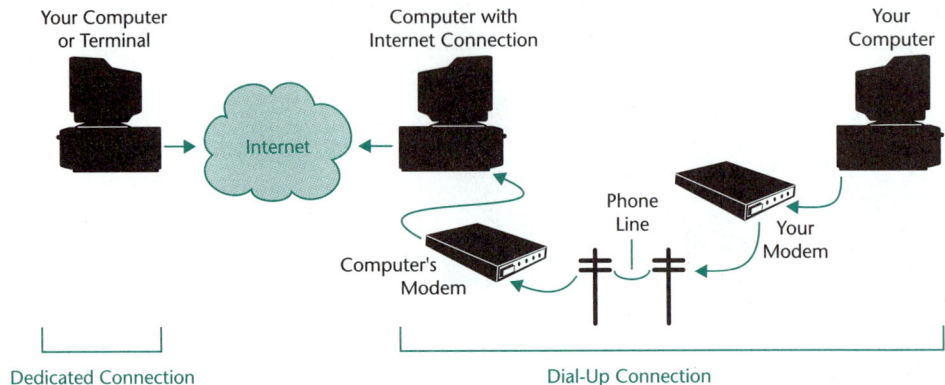

Your Computer or Terminal

Computer with Internet Connection

Your Computer

Internet

Phone Line

Your Modem

Computer's Modem

Dedicated Connection

Dial-Up Connection

does not even require you to have a personal computer. Rather, you can use a **terminal** that has no processing power but can be used to send and receive information from the terminal to a computer.

Because of the high cost, dedicated connections are usually only available at educational institutions, such as the University of Iowa and Harvard University, and large commercial organizations, such as Bell Labs, AT&T, and the Microsoft Corporation. The University of Kansas pays about $35,000 per year to make a direct connection through a large service provider, an amount that few individual Internet aspirants could afford. The large institutional connection, in turn, becomes a connection for thousands of people who work at or attend that institution.

Dial-Up Connections

Dial-up connections become available when large organizations that have a dedicated connection make the connection available to its members. If you are a student, faculty member, researcher, or employee of a university or institution that has a connection to the Internet, then you've got one too. This is the primary way that most of you will connect. You will dial up or connect from a terminal in a lab to your university's host computer which, in turn, has a dedicated connection to the Internet.

Commercial Internet Providers

A **commercial Internet provider** is another type of dial-up connection. With the tremendous growth the Internet is experiencing, the publicity it has received, and the relatively limited access by individuals who do not work or study at places that have dedicated connections, commercial services are now providing connections to the Internet for people who have no other way to gain access.

Using a commercial Internet provider is just like using a dedicated line, except for the fact that the dedicated line belongs to a host who charges you to use it. They provide you with a phone connection that gives you access to their computer which accesses the Internet through a dedicated line. It also usually provides all the software you need and technical support as well, although this can vary greatly depending upon the provider. In turn, you pay a sign-up fee and/or a monthly fee and/or an hourly fee. The competition continues to heat up and there are some great deals available with more Internet providers coming on-line almost daily. A good place to find out about who's offering what is to look at WIRED and Internet World, two periodicals widely available.

The quality and offerings of service providers vary greatly. Some service providers currently have access to only the most basic of Internet services such as mail. Others provide lots of different service options, such as mail, downloading of files, searching of databases and more. Those that have limited offerings, however, probably won t be around very long since consumers are demanding full-featured Internet tools for their hard-earned money. If you're considering a service provider for your connection, who should you turn to and what should you consider?

How to Select a Service Provider

There are 100 service providers available in the United States. In Table 2.1, you can find the names and address of five different commercial Internet providers and a summary of their services so that you can easily make a comparison of features such as cost and technical support. This table illustrates how services differ from one another. Use it as a guide when you contact other providers to compare additional information.

You can expect a commercial service to charge a monthly fee, maybe a sign-up fee, and maybe a fee for the amount of time you are connected to the host computer. If the service provider does not provide a local phone call to make the initial contact to sign on to their computer, there will also be the cost of the call itself. Even when the commercial Internet provider uses a special long distance company such as SprintNet, this phone time costs about $8 more per hour.

There are some good deals out there, particularly if you belong to a professional or trade group. For example, Pipeline is a commercial Internet provider in the New York City area. Currently, they charge $10 for five hours of free time including software that makes the Net user-friendly for members of the Author's Guild. You can buy additional hours for $2 each. Or, you can pay $35 a month for unlimited use.

If you live in the Washington, D.C., area there's another good deal waiting for you. The International Internet Association is offering free access to the Internet. Even if you don't live in that area and have to pay for a long-distance call, they have an 800 number that is available for .20 per minute or $12 per hour. Contact them for more information at (202) 387-5445 or write to them at The International Internet Society, Suite 852, 2020 Pennsylvania Avenue, NW, Washington, DC 20006.

Which Internet services commercial providers offer varies greatly and is changing every day. Call or write these service providers to learn what they

TABLE 2.1 A comparison of some commercial Internet providers.

		Service				
		Panix	**Digex**	**CERFnet**	**The WELL**	**The Pipeline**
		(212) 741-4400 (voice) 9212 741-5311 (fax) e-mail to staff@panix.com	(310) 847-5100 (voice) (310) 847-5215 (fax) e-mail to info@digex.net	POB 84608 San Diego, CA 92186 (800) 876-2373 (voice) (619) 455-3900 (fax) e-mail to help@cerf.net	27 Gate 5 Road Sausalito, CA 94965 (415) 332-4335 e-mail to info@well.sf.ca.us	150 Broadway New York, NY 10038 (212) 267-3636 e-mail to info@pipeline.com
# of Customers	Approximate number of users	?	5,000	20,000	11,000	more than 1,000
On-line technical support?	Here you can actually speak to a human being and ask questions and hopefully get answers.	yes	yes	yes	yes	
Real live people support?	All services offer some kind of on-line support with varying hours.	no	yes	yes	yes	yes, voice mailbox
Bulletin board for technical support?	At the least, each service allows you to leave e-mail for their technical people to answer.	yes	yes	yes	yes	yes
Connect fee?	This is the fee that is charged for every hour you are connected to the service.	none	after 6 hours per day, $1 per hour	$20 per month, plus $5 per hour	$2 per hour	basic plan is $35 for unlimited use
Sign-up/set-up fee?	This is the initial fee for signing up and becoming a member.	basic Internet account is $20 per month	$20 set-up and $25 per month	$50	$15 per month	none
Do you provide front end software?	This is the rate that is charged for non-prime time use.	no	no	yes	yes	no
Local phone connections?	Some services have local phone lines available, some use special sharing networks such as SprintNet, and some are only available in limited geographical areas.	phone connections are available in the local New York City area	generally available locally and on the East coast	800 number is available as well as local access numbers in selected areas	various local numbers in large cities, plus access through networks	all Internet services are available
What Internet services do you provide?	Some companies only provide mail or news, while others provide everything including the Web.	all Internet services are available	all Internet services are available	all Internet services are available	all Internet services are available	

Note that all these providers, and almost every other provider, offer all the vital Internet features such as ftp, telnet, and news and have an address for sending mail to get answers to inquiries. A ? in the chart indicates that the company did not provide the requested information.

TABLE 2.2 Questions you should ask when looking for a commercial Internet provider.

How much will this cost?

1. What is the hourly connect charge, if any?
2. Is there a sign-up or start-up fee? Is it one time or annual?
3. What is the monthly fee?
4. What is the hourly charge?
5. Is there a discounted hourly charge for after-hours or weekend connections?
6. Is there a discount for volume use?
7. Are there different costs for different speed modems?
8. Are there discounts for members of particular organizations?

What does the service offer?

1. What basic services (such as telnet, ftp, etc.) are provided?
2. Does the service provide access to other commercial services (so you can e-mail your friends and colleagues who are not on the same service)?
3. Are there different types of accounts available, at different rates for different categories of users such as individuals, companies, etc.? What about members who want to just send mail?
4. What modem speeds are available and is there a different charge for each speed?
5. What software is available for connecting to the Internet?
6. How many customers do you have?
7. Is there a local phone line in my area for me to connect? If not, how will I connect from a remote site and how much will it cost?
8. Does the service offer storage space for downloaded files? How much space? What does it cost to keep things in storage?
9. Is free software provided for working with the Internet?
10. Are there practice or tutorial exercises available? Is there a cost for the use of these?

What about technical support?

1. Is on-line technical support available?
2. Is phone support available?
3. Is there a charge for phone support? Is there an 800 number?
4. Does tech support offer a forum on any major bulletin boards so I can connect and ask my questions that way?

offer. After the next chapter you can e-mail them for information! Table 2.2 lists some questions you should ask any service provider before you sign on.

Along with your computer, you need an **account.** Having an account provides you with access to the network you need to connect to the Internet. Think of an account as a key to a door. In this case, the door is the Internet.

Where do these Internet accounts come from? They are usually assigned to new users and managed by a local Internet boss such as a system administrator or from the commercial provider to which you have subscribed. We'll assume that you have a valid account. If not, ask your teacher or system administrator to assign you one or tell you how to get one.

INTERNET AND YOUR COMPUTER

The Internet and the protocols it use make it possible for virtually any computer with communications software to access the Internet. Dedicated connections don't need much more than a terminal to access the Internet. Dial-up users need both software and hardware.

To connect, dial-up users must have at least the following:

- A **modem** to **modulate** and **demodulate** data so it can be transferred over telephone lines. A modem is a hardware tool that *modulates*, or converts digital signals to audio signals so the information can be transmitted over the phone line. The modem on the receiving end of the line *demodulates*, or converts the audio signals back to digital ones so the receiving computer can understand the message.

  The faster the modem, the faster the information is transferred. However, fast modems are more expensive to use than slow ones because some Internet providers charge more per hour for the faster modem, which transfers or accesses more information more quickly. These days you can never buy a modem that's too fast. If you can afford it, go for a modem that has a transfer rate of 14,400 bits per second (bps), much faster than the old modems that could only transfer at a 300 bps rate. As an added bonus, many of these 14,400 modems double as fax modems.

- **Telecommunications software**, such as Procomm, Cross Talk, or MicroPhone, converts signals so they can be sent through a modem to the host computer and allows your computer to connect to the network through which you will access the Internet. You may also need a SLIP connection. **SLIP** stands for **Serial Line Internet Protocol**. This is a method for connecting to the Internet that makes the Net think that you are a direct connection rather than someone dialing in to connect through another computer.

- Software for using the Internet allows you to use the Internet. Telecommunications software allows you to connect to the Internet network. Some companies, such as Pipeline and America Online, give away easy-to-use software packages to help sign up new members and make it easy to use the Internet.

- Sufficient storage or hard disk space is needed so that Internet software can be stored and used and other files can be saved. Remember, a significant part of your Internet activity can involve transferring files from a host computer to your computer. Computers at most colleges and universities have more than enough room to store these new files. If you are connecting from home, make sure that your personal computer has enough storage space as well.

  The first personal computers came with hard drives that had only 10 megabytes (MB) of storage space. Today that's hardly enough to store an application such as WordPerfect. The larger the storage device, the cheaper it costs per megabyte. Try to get a hard drive that is at least 400 MB in size. Buy the hard disk with the most storage space you can afford.

- Temporary or internal memory called **RAM (random access memory)** is used to perform all the jobs you want your computer to do. RAM provides space for the computer to carry out its instructions. Four megabytes is probably sufficient, but the more the better, especially if you want to have several applications open at once.

Your modem and software have to work smoothly for any Internet connection to be successful. Fortunately, mail-order computer vendors, such as Compaq, Dell, and Zeos as well as your local superstore have such systems with all the components (modem, software, etc.) configured and ready to go. Many complete systems also come with the software you need to connect to commercial Net providers (such as America Online, CompuServe, or Prodigy). Many commercial providers sell modems at a reduced price.

NAMES AND ADDRESSES

Think of the Internet as a bunch of major streets that connect lots of different neighborhoods. Within the neighborhoods are other streets where people live in houses and apartments. Each house and apartment has a street number. These numbers are known as addresses.

This is a simplified example, but the address analogy works pretty well for the Internet. Every connection to the Internet has its own unique number. In fact, each connection actually has two different forms of address. The first is an **Internet Protocol** or **IP address** and the second is a **domain name**, a character-based name that represents an Internet location. Let's see how these addresses are used by the Internet and how they are distinguished from each other.

Internet Protocol or IP Addresses

People who design computers and the systems that operate them love numbers, because numbers convey lots of information in a small amount of space. After all, that's why computers work so fast—they transform everything (such as text, graphics, and sound) into numbers.

So it's no surprise that one way to assign an Internet address to a computer is with a number called the Internet Protocol or IP address. The IP address is a set of four numbers separated by periods, such as 129.237.34.1, which is the IP address for a connection at the University of Kansas.

Each of the four numbers that constitutes an IP address represents some characteristics of that location. The numbers are arranged in hierarchical order. For example, the first number in the sequence (129) tells the Internet what network the computer is part of.

In Figure 2.2, you can see an IP address broken down by each individual digit or set of digits separated by periods. Working toward the right, 237 represents a network or a host located within the network numbered 129, and so on until you end up with a specific host computer (represented by the number 1 in Figure 2.2). This is the specific computer you use to enter and receive data

FIGURE 2.2

The components of
an Internet Protocol
(or IP) address.

For the IP Address 129.237.34.1. here's what each number means.

129	237	34	1
first-level domain number	subdomain number	subdomain number	host name number

across the Internet. The IP address is created by assigning numbers to Internet connections.

Domain Names

IP addresses can be difficult to remember. In response to this potential problem, the **Domain Name System** is used to assign text characters to each IP address. Just as any one computer on the Internet has a unique IP number associated with it, it also has a unique domain name.

There are several differences between IP addresses and domain names. IP addresses are assigned so that the *leftmost* number encompasses the largest category of computers in the network. In a domain name, the top of the hierarchy is the *rightmost* set of characters. For example, the domain name for one of the computers at the University of Kansas, named falcon, is falcon.cc.ukans.edu. As you can see, the rightmost part of that four-part address (also separated by periods) is edu, the broadest element in the name, signifying an educational institution.

The complete domain name is known as the **Fully Qualified Domain Name** (or **FQDN**). The FQDN for the University of Kansas is falcon.cc.ukans.edu. Figure 2.3 shows what each element of some FQDNs represents.

FIGURE 2.3

The elements of
domain names.

Here's what each part of the FQDN falcon.cc.ukans.edu represents.

Element	What it means
falcon	the name of the computer
cc	the subdomain that stands for computer center
ukans	the domain name that stands for University of Kansas
edu	the type of site

Here's what each part of the FQDN mit.edu represents.

Element	What it means
mit	the domain name that stands for the Massachusetts Institute of Technology
edu	the type of site

Here's what each part of the FQDN compuserve.com represents.

Element	What it means
compuserve	the domain name that stands for CompuServe
com	the type of site

The FQDN for the Massachusetts Institute of Technology is mit.edu; the FQDN for CompuServe is compuserve.com. As you see, not all domain names (such as mit.edu) have four parts (unlike their IP address counterpart). Unlike IP numbers, there is no universal system for a domain name. The system administrator assigns the name for the host computer (such as ukans). The other parts are assigned by the administrative unit within the organization. So cc represents computer center and falcon represents the name of the computer. A domain name with fewer components (such as mit.edu) means that the organization uses a **router**, or a separate system to transfer data to its destination.

When you see a domain name, you can tell what the organization belongs to by looking at the letters to the right of the last period in the domain name, the highest level of the hierarchy. Table 2.3 lists the different endings to FQDNs and what these endings represent.

TABLE 2.3 Domain types on the Internet.

End of Domain Name	Type of Organization	Example	Organization
com	commercial organization	compuserve.com	CompuServe
edu	educational organization	falcon.cc.ukans.edu	University of Kansas
gov	government organization	whitehouse.gov	White House
mil	military organization	gordon.army.mil	Army
org	Some other organization that does not fit into any of the above	ahkcus.org	Chinese Poem Exchange Network
net	network resource and information centers	archie.sura.net	a Net indexing system housed at the University of Maryland

There are many country names that you might find attached to the end of a domain name as well, such as ca for Canada, fr for France, and uk for the United Kingdom. Table 2.4 shows a list of 24 country codes.

Your User Name

Add one more piece to the puzzle and then you'll know all about Internet names and addresses. That's the piece that goes before the Fully Qualified Domain Name. It is almost always separated from the Fully Qualified Domain Name by an **at sign** which looks like this: @. Whereas Fully Qualified Domain Names are assigned by institutions, the **user name** is provided by the user, usually when that person first gets an account. Sometimes, the account (such as njs) is the same as the user name. There are no Internet guidelines for assigning user

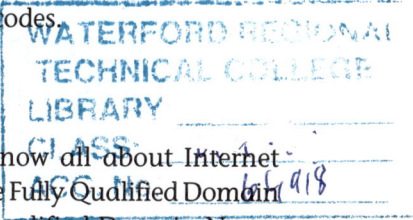

TABLE 2.4 Country codes used on the Internet.

Country	Code	Country	Code
Argentina	ar	Italy	it
Australia	au	Kuwait	kw
Bahamas	bs	Mali	ml
Belgium	be	Morocco	ma
Brazil	br	Nigeria	ng
Canada	ca	Peru	pe
Chile	cl	Romania	ro
Costa Rica	cr	Slovakia	sl
Egypt	eg	Sweden	se
France	fr	United Kingdom	ae
Hong Kong	hk	United States	us
Israel	il	Zimbabwe	zw

names. People most often use some combination of their initials and full names such as billl for Billy Lerner, sfg for Samuel Franklin Green, and so on.

For example, my colleague Sam's complete address at the University of Kansas is sgf@kuhub.ukans.edu. His user name is sgt followed by an @ sign, followed by the domain name for the University of Kansas, the specific computer on the network and educational institution (edu). Sam selected the user name sfg. The system administrator at the University of Kansas assigned the kuhub.ukans.edu.

My friend's address at CompuServe is 70404.365@compuserve.com. Her user name is 70404.365 (assigned by CompuServe, as is usually the case for commercial Internet providers), and the domain name for Compuserve is compuserve.com. I can reach Ed at Apple Computer at edmr@apple.com.

Now that you know about domain names, and we hope you have found out what yorus is, can you tell by looking at a domain name where the computer is located? Basically, the answer is no. The same computer can have different domain names, but have the same IP address. Moreover, the name might have nothing to do with the location. For example, the address apple.com is at Apple Computer, which is pretty obvious. But what about loc.gov.? That's the address of the Library of Congress. Once you see it, it becomes obvious. How about orstu.edu (Oregon State University) or dg.com (Data General)? The addresses become obvious only when you know what they represent.

Can you ever tell who the address belongs to just by looking at the domain name? Probably not until you become accustomed to using domain names. As you work on the Internet, you will use domain names that may seem a bit cryptic, but they all lead to a place that has a name. You'll find yourself recognizing which domain name represents which location. You'll become familiar with some often-used domain names that you'll memorize as you work.

USING PASSWORDS

Each time you connect to the Internet, you will be asked to identify yourself. You do this by providing an account name or number (often your user name) and your **password**. Passwords are designed to protect your account from unauthorized use. No one should know your password except you and the system administrator. You don't want anyone else representing you, which is exactly what happens when someone else logs on under your name. If you are paying to use a commercial system and someone logs on using your account number and password, you are paying for another person's connect time which can be very expensive. A good system administrator will not even tell you what your own password is. If you forget it, the system administrator will probably assign you a new one after being sure of your identity.

Some golden rules about password use are:

- Don't give your password to anyone.

- Change your password about every two weeks.

- Write your password down and keep it somewhere safe so you can refer to it if necessary. Don't leave it lying around. Some security analysts think that writing it down is a bad practice because someone can find and use it. They may be right. On the other hand, if you are prone to forgetting things, or if you have access to several systems and need several passwords, better to be safe than sorry. If you lose or forget it, your system administrator might be able to help you. In some cases, even the system operator cannot be of any help.

- Be sure that your password contains both numerals and text characters such as 2K66HW, instead of 423467 or THGYRF, so that it is less easy to guess should someone try. Some systems require that passwords begin with a number. You should check with your system administrator or your teacher to see if there are specific guidelines for passwords.

- Don't use the obvious choices for your password. Your home address, phone number, children's names, or boyfriend's shoe size are all less preferable than a more unique collection of characters.

- Don't use letters that are adjacent to each other on the keyboard such as asdf or that form a pattern such as a1b2c3.

- Find out if your system is case sensitive to passwords; that is, if THGYRF and THGyRF are considered different.

- Make sure your password is at least 6 characters long.

You've got a great jump on the basics and have some understanding of what you need to connect to the Internet and what options for connecting exist. If you have an account number, you now have an understanding of what it means and how it is used throughout the Internet system. Now it's time to move on to the most basic and exciting element within the Internet—using the World Wide Web (or WWW) browser, Netscape. We guarantee you an "I can't stop experience!"

KEY WORDS

@ or at sign
account
commercial Internet provider
dedicated connection
demodulate
dial-up connection
domain name
Domain Name System
Fully Qualified Domain Name (FQDN)
Intenet Protocol or IP address

modem
modulate
password
random access memory (RAM)
router
Serial Line Internet Protocol (SLIP)
telecommunications software
terminal
user name

REVIEW QUESTIONS

1. You're a home computer enthusiast who wants to use the Internet, and you're lucky enough to be a student at a major university that already has a direct connection to the Internet. What do you need to connect?

2. What are some of the advantages and disadvantages of a commercial Internet provider?

3. What are the differences between an IP address and a domain name?

4. What's wrong with the following passwords: neil, abcdef, and Internet? How would you change them to make them acceptable?

5. What are the standard components of an Internet FQDN?

6. Who is responsible for assigning accounts? What factors does that person need to consider in the assignment of accounts?

EXPLORATION EXERCISES

1. What is the IP address for any of the computers at your university or business that have a direct connection to the Internet? Find out what each element in the IP address or the domain name represents.

2. Find ten other FQDNs, from other departments at your school, other schools and businesses, and individuals in your local community. For each address, identify the user name and the elements in the domain name. How are they similar? How are they different?

3. Contact any two Internet providers (you can call or use U.S. mail) and ask them to send you information about their Internet offerings. When you get the material, compare the services to determine which one offers Internet features such as telnet, mail, and news.

4. Suppose you are the system administrator at a large university where all FDQNs end with edu. Assign FQDNs to ten friends. What system did you use to assign user names or allow them to be assigned? How did you select the domain name? How does the domain name differ from others that your classmates might have selected?

3

An Introduction to the World Wide Web and Netscape

After completing this chapter, you'll be able to

- Understand what a home page is
- Go to new home pages
- Use the bookmark and history features of Netscape
- Use the various Netscape menu options
- Explore the World Wide Web
- Understand the basics of HTML language

In Chapter 2, we introduced you to basic Internet terms and concepts, including how the Internet is accessed, what commercial Internet providers offer, and how Internet names and addresses work. Now we're ready to actually explore the Internet and use what many people find the most appealing aspect of the Internet—the **World Wide Web**.

You already know that the Internet is a network of networks. The World Wide Web (or **WWW**) is a collection of documents representing different locations that are linked to one another. Clicking on a particular word, picture, or sound in one document can quickly take you to another. On the Web, you'll find what are called **distributed hypertext documents**. These documents, also called **home pages**, contain **hot links** that connect one home page to another. In order to see and use these home pages and hot links, you need a browser. And that's exactly where Netscape comes in. Netscape is a browser that can be used for exploring the WWW, as can other browsers such as Mosaic and Cello. We selected Netscape for this book because it is available on-line so that you can try it out for free before you register and pay; it is widely available; and it is being used by more people than any other browser. Besides that, it is easy to use and lots of fun. So get ready to browse and meet the World Wide Web.

HOW TO START NETSCAPE

The installation of Netscape on your system depends upon more factors than we can cover it here but, basically, it's installed like any Windows application where you use the install.exe command and then create a new item using Program Manager. When you do this, the Netscape icon ![N] will appear on your screen. Double-click on the icon and you should see the Netscape opening screen as shown in Figure 3.1. Unless you have a direct connection to the Internet, you may also need a SLIP connection. A **SLIP connection** makes your computer operate as if it were a direct connection. If you are working in a school lab, this has most likely been taken care of. If not, it's best to get some help from a computer science major, your instructor, or someone who has already installed Netscape.

FIGURE 3.1

The Netscape opening screen.

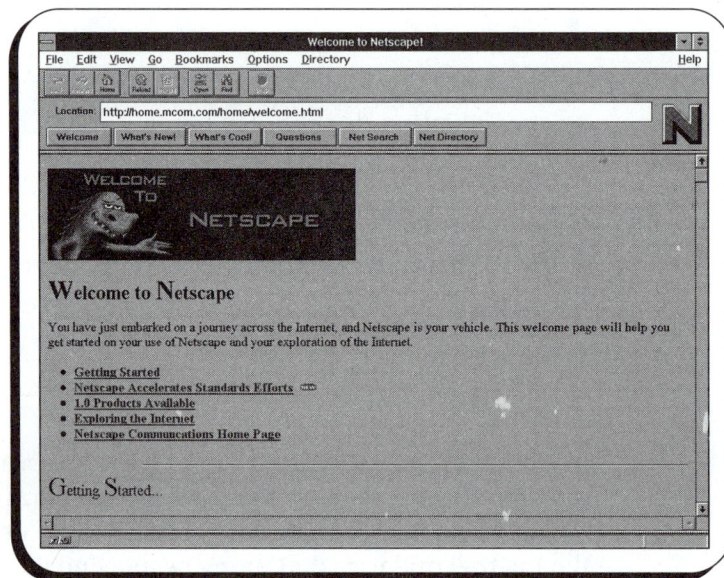

ALL ABOUT HOME PAGES

A home page is a collection of information; all home pages contain similar characteristics. You can get to different home pages in a variety of ways. We will explain how later in this chapter and you'll also learn how to create your own home page. Let's start by exploring the opening home page for the Library of Congress shown in Figure 3.2.

FIGURE 3.2

The home page
for the Library
of Congress

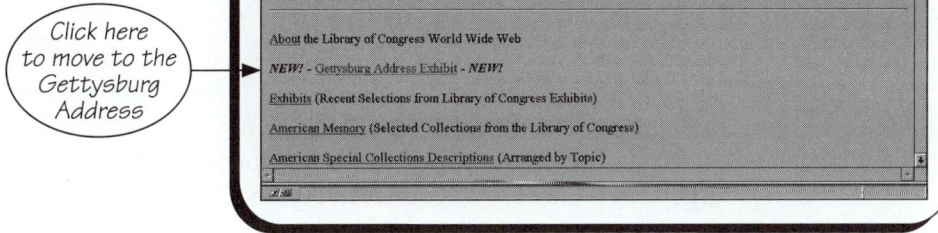

*Click here
to move to the
Gettysburg
Address*

At the top of the page, you can see the title The Library of Congress World Wide Web Home Page which tells you what the current home page is. Below the title of the home page is a set of pull-down menus (File, Edit, View, Go, Bookmarks, Options, Directory, and Help). These offer important features for using Netscape and we'll discuss each one later in this chapter. Below the menus are the Netscape Toolbar and Toolbar buttons (Back, Forward, Home, Reload, Images, Open Find, and Stop). These perform specific functions described later in this chapter.

The Location: text box indicates the location of the active home page. This is an address on the WWW and is also called a **URL** for **universal resource locator**. Once you know the URL for a particular home page, enter it in the Location: text box, press Enter, and Netscape will take you there. Sooner or later you will notice that all URLs begin with the characters **http**, or **hypertext transfer protocol**. HTTP is the system used by the Web to transfer data from the Internet to your computer. Below the Location: text box is a set of directory buttons that contain links to pages with additoinal information. Net Search and Net Directory are special tools for exploring the Internet.

The contents of the home page start with a graphic of the Library of Congress. Below the graphic is a list of highlighted words (such as About the Library of Congress World Wide Web) that are links to other pages. When you place the mouse pointer on one of these highlighted words, the pointer changes to a hand shape About the Library of Congress World Wide Web . When you click on one of these highlighted words, you are taken to a new page. Once you go to the new page, the color of the highlighted word you clicked on will change to indicate that you have already used this link. You can click on it as many times as you like; Netscape is just reminding you where you've been. On most systems, the highlighted words (and images) are blue. Once clicked, they turn purple. (This color scheme may be different for your computer and Internet arrangements.)

The status indicator, located at the bottom of the Netscape window, indicates when a transfer is taking place. Figure 3.3 hows that information is being transferred from a remote location to your Internet connection.

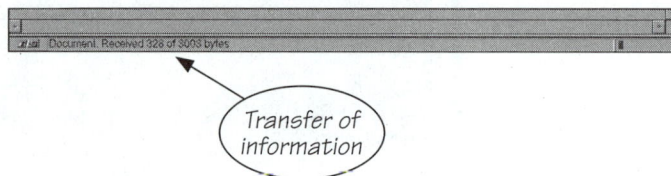

Transfer of information

The **status bar** also shows you the location (or URL) for a page you can link to when you place the mouse pointer on a highlighted word in a home page. For example, if you were in the Library of Congress home page (which you will go to in a moment) and placed the mouse pointer on the highlighted Gettysburg Address Exhibit (as you see in Figure 3.2), the status bar would show

```
http://lcweb.loc.gov/exhibits/G.Address/ga.html
```

By their nature, URLs are cryptic and it's tough to tell where one is physically located or which institution is sponsoring the home page. It would be handy to keep a running list of the URLs you like and want to visit again. That's exactly what the Bookmark pull-down menu does, which we'll explain later in this chapter.

Finally, on the status bar, is a **progress bar** that indicates when the transfer process is complete. You can watch this bar and see how quickly data is being transferred from the Net to your computer. Keep in mind that since pictures contain loads of information, home pages with pictures will take longer to transfer.

LINKING TO ANOTHER HOME PAGE

Here we go. You should be at the Netscape home page with a URL of

```
http://home.mcom.home/welcome.html
```

To go to the Library of Congress, follow these steps.

1. Using regular windows procedures, highlight the home page address in the Location: text box so that it appears in reverse video as you see in Figure 3.4.

2. Type http://lcweb.loc.gov/homepage/lchp.html and press Enter.

FIGURE 3.4
Highlighting the
current location.

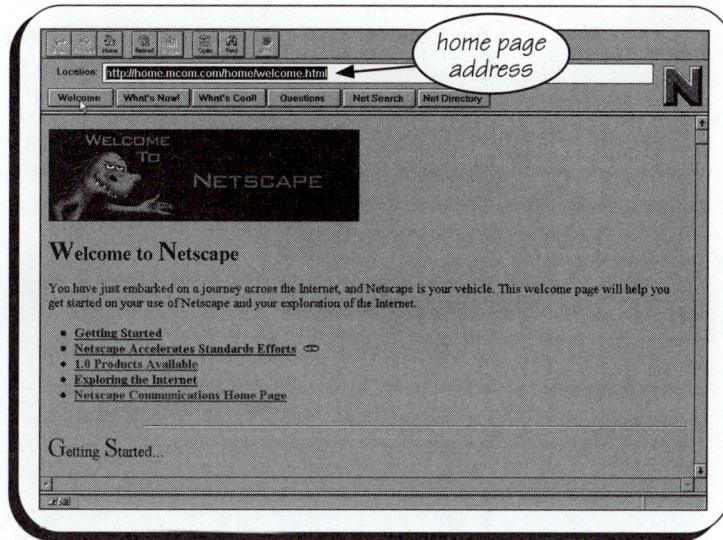

You must type the address exactly as you see it here and you may have to keep case (upper- and lowercase characters) consistent as well. If you don't, you may see a message such as

```
!Unable to locate host
```

It is very easy to mistype characters that make no inherent sense (such as http or HTML); be careful. After the data is transferred to your machine, you should find yourself at the Library of Congress home page. You should be able to see the links (or underlined words) on the page as well.

That's all there is to going to a new home page by entering a new URL. Another way to get to a different home page is by clicking on any of the high-lighted words or graphics that are available on the home page you are looking at. Follow these steps as we go to the Gettysburg Exhibit. Keep in mind that home pages are always changing—what you see in these pages might not match what you see on your monitor. If there is a difference, don't be too concerned. Try to work through the material to learn the techniques. Besides, working on your own, you are sure to discover interesting sites to share with your classmates.

1. Locate the *New!*–Gettysburg Address Exhibit–*New!*
2. Place the mouse pointer on the highlighted words.
3. Click once. Netscape will then begin transferring the data. The next home page you see should look like Figure 3.5.

FIGURE 3.5
The Gettysburg
Address
home page.

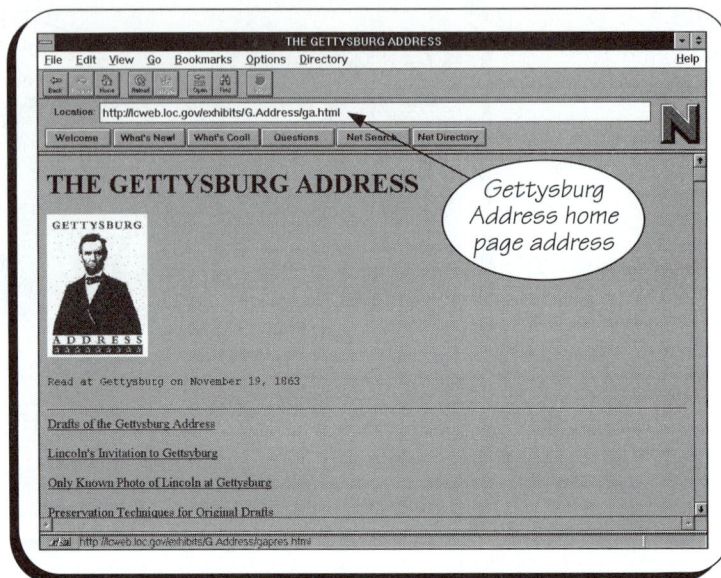

Now it's time for a BIG and important warning. Parts of the Internet change daily and even hourly, in both structure and content. The Internet is a dynamic arena for information dissemination. Because of this, the home page that you see may not look like ours; and in fact, it may no longer be available. Nonetheless, most of the basic principles we are illustrating hold true no matter which home page you are looking at in Netscape. If you do not see the particular home page that we are featuring and cannot easily follow along, ask your instructor to help you find for another home page which will allow you to follow along.

If you scroll down one page, you can see that there is a host of other places you can link to such as

```
Drafts of the Gettysburg Address
Lincoln's Invitation to Gettysburg
Only Known Photo of Lincoln at Gettysburg
```

and much more. And what is so terrific about Netscape and the Web is that all these resources are only a click away.

USING BOOKMARKS AND HISTORY

Even if you're not a Civil War buff, you may want to make it easy to return to whichever home page you are currently on and also to view the history of all the home pages you have visited during a Netscape session. You can do this quite easily using Bookmarks and the View History option on the Go menu.

A **bookmark** in Netscape is similar to a bookmark in a book. It keeps your place until you return later and want to start reading from where you stopped; it allows you to personalize your Netscape activities. To create a bookmark, follow these steps.

1. Be sure you are in the home page that you want to create a bookmark for.
2. Click Bookmarks, and then click Add Bookmark. You can also use the Ctrl+A key combination to add a bookmark.

The title of the home page (e.g., Library of Congress World Wide Web home page) will be added to your list of bookmarks. Figure 3.6 shows the list of bookmarks that have been added to the Bookmarks menu. All you need to do is scroll down and select the bookmark you want and Netscape will deliver you to that URL as soon as possible.

FIGURE 3.6
A list of bookmarks.

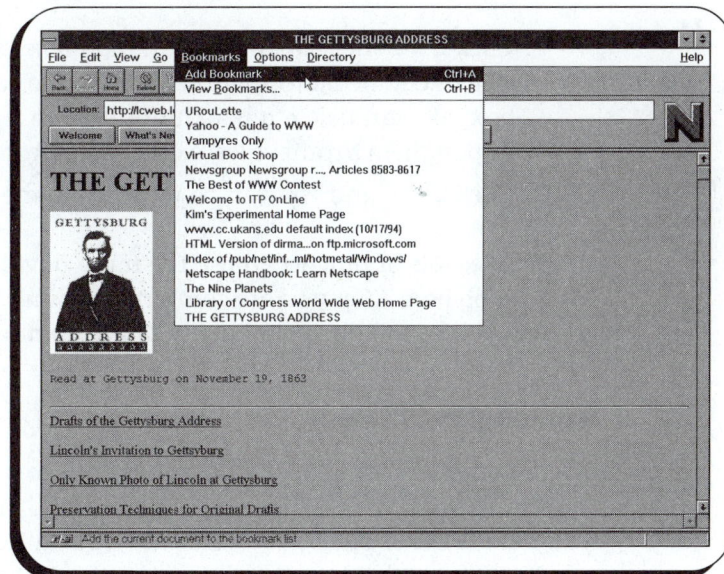

Advanced Bookmark Stuff

Once you have created a list of bookmarks, you may want to do more than just view them. While the advanced features of working with bookmarks are beyond the scope of this book, you should know where these tools are located so that you can at least see some of the possibilities. All of these advanced tools are located on the View Bookmark option on the Bookmarks menu. Follow these steps to access them.

1. Click Bookmarks, and then click View Bookmark. When you do this, you will see the Bookmark List as shown in Figure 3.7.

FIGURE 3.7

The bookmark list.

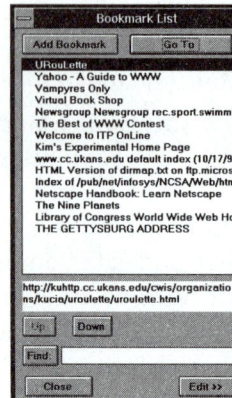

2. Click Edit. The Bookmark List dialog box expands to include options as well as detailed information about the selected bookmark. In this dialog box you can delete a bookmark (Remove Item), create new bookmarks, import them to other files, export them from other files, and much more.

3. Click Close and you will be returned to the active home page.

It takes lots of practice to use the more advanced features of the Bookmark List dialog box. After you are comfortable using Netscape and the basic commands, you can explore working with bookmarks on your own.

Viewing the History

There's another way to get around from page to page besides using bookmarks and that's through the View History command on the Go menu. This provides you with a list of places you've been—your history using Netscape—and an easy way to get back to them. To view the history of your Netscape session, follow these steps.

1. Click Go.

2. Click View History. You will see a History dialog box as shown in Figure 3.8 that lists the title of the pages you have seen as well as the corresponding URL for each of them. You can double-click on a page title to go to that page, or highlight a page and then click on the Go To button, or create a bookmark for that page by highlighting the page title and then clicking the Create Bookmark button. Keep in mind that the View History dialog box only shows where you have been. It is not a record of your bookmarks—you can visit a home page without adding it to your bookmark list.

FIGURE 3.8
Viewing the history
of home pages.

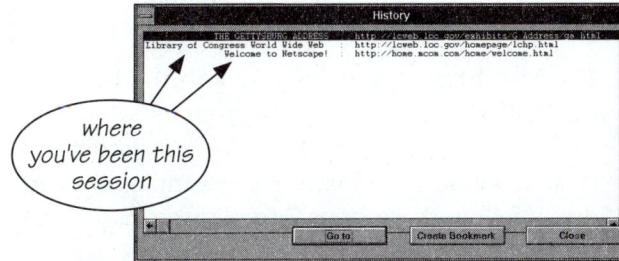

You have now learned enough to begin serious exploration of the WWW using Netscape. That's not to say you're an expert, but you should be able to locate pages, go to them, save their location as bookmarks, and return to them at a later time.

WHERE TO FIND HOME PAGES

This is *the* $64,000 question. To begin with, you have to understand that anyone can create a home page—more about this later. As there is no central listing of home pages, you cannot go to a directory or other source such as "All the Home Pages on the World Wide Web" since the Web, and the number of pages on it, are changing so rapidly. Although many trade books offer different listings, some of this listings are out of date before the books are published.

The best way to find home pages is to explore the Web and talk with your friends and colleagues to find out what they're discovering. And, when you find a terrific home page, save its location as a bookmark and share that information with a friend. If you have the time now, there is one home page you should explore named URouLette. This home page, created at the University of Kansas, allows you to click on a roulette wheel (what else?) and then takes you to a different home page. Which one? It selects at random—you might find yourself at a home page on X-rays in Ugandan or Solar and Stellar physics at Harvard (http://CFA-www.harvard.edu/CFA/ssp.html) or Point Grey Mini School in Vancouver, Canada (http://trinculo.educ.sfu.ca/pgm/pgmhome.html) or Gleanings from the Writings of Baha'u'llah (http//:www.cs.cornell.edu/ Info/People/kalantar/Writings/Bahaullah/GWB/sec-24.h tml). By now you probably want the URL for URouLette, right? Here's how to get to it; more about this URL later.

```
http://kuhttp.cc.ukans.edu/vwis/organizations/kucia/uroulette/
uroulette.html
```

THE NETSCAPE MENUS

As with any Windows application, Netscape offers a set of menus and commands that dictate how you use Netscape and what it does. Let's talk about what each of the seven menus in Figure 3.1 offers. We'll discuss the features you are most likely to select and those that have the most utility.

The File Menu: Going to Other Home Pages

The **File menu** provides you with the tools to create a new window, open a new URL location, open a file from a dialog box, save a file, save a link to disk, mail a document, produce information about the current home page, print, close a window, and exit. For example, to print a copy of the Gettysburg Address, follow these steps. We assume that you are in the Gettysburg Address home page. The URL is

```
http://lcweb.loc.gov/exhibits/G.Address/gfa.html
```

1. Click on Drafts of the Gettysburg Address.
2. Click on Transcript of the Nicolay Draft of the Gettysburg Address.
3. Click File and then click Print. The home page containing the Gettysburg Address should print.

It's as simple as that. Or, if you wanted to save the page to a file so that you can work with the text or use the text in another document, follow these steps. We assume that you are in the home page showing the actual words in the Gettysburg Address.

1. Click File and then click Save As. A typical Save dialog box will appear.
2. Locate the disk and directory where you want to save the text.
3. Click OK. Remember, the Gettysburg home page may look different, but that should not stop you from practicing these skills.

The Edit Menu: Finding Information

The **Edit menu** provides you with the tools to undo previous operations, find information and cut, copy and paste from one location to another. For example, you may want to find mention of the word *freedom* in the Gettysburg Address. To find information on a home page, follow these steps.

1. Click Edit, then click Find. You'll see the Find dialog box as shown in Figure 3.9.

FIGURE 3.9

The Find dialog box.

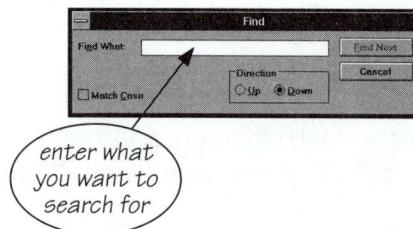

enter what you want to search for

2. Enter freedom in the text box.

3. Click OK.

Netscape will find the first occurrence of the word *freedom*. Unlike this example, some home pages are very large—the ability to search for information can be a great help.

The View Menu: Seeing What Makes a Home Page

The **View menu** provides you with tools to reload the current home page, load the images in a home page where you can see them (which is the default), refresh the screen with a fresh copy of the home page, and produce a listing of the source code of what a home page actually looks like. For example, in Figure 3.10, you can view the source code for the Netscape opening screen you saw in Figure 3.1. To see it, follow the steps below.

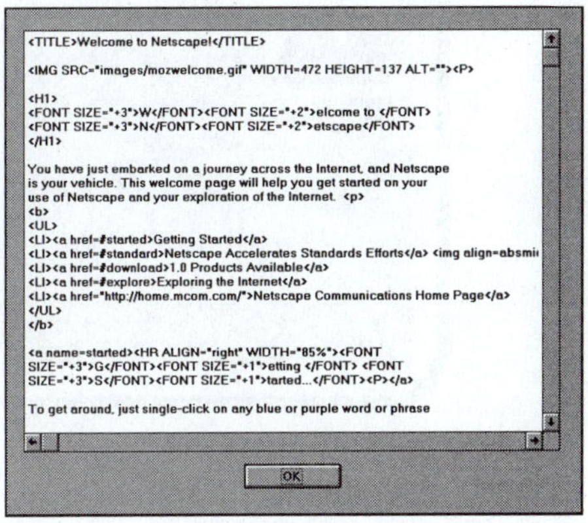

FIGURE 3.10

The source code for the Netscape opening screen.

```
<TITLE>Welcome to Netscape!</TITLE>

<IMG SRC="images/mozwelcome.gif" WIDTH=472 HEIGHT=137 ALT=""><P>

<H1>
<FONT SIZE="+3">W</FONT><FONT SIZE="+2">elcome to </FONT>
<FONT SIZE="+3">N</FONT><FONT SIZE="+2">etscape</FONT>
</H1>

You have just embarked on a journey across the Internet, and Netscape
is your vehicle. This welcome page will help you get started on your
use of Netscape and your exploration of the Internet.  <p>
<b>
<UL>
<LI><a href=#started>Getting Started</a>
<LI><a href=#standard>Netscape Accelerates Standards Efforts</a> <img align=absmi
<LI><a href=#download>1.0 Products Available</a>
<LI><a href=#explore>Exploring the Internet</a>
<LI><a href="http://home.mcom.com/">Netscape Communications Home Page</a>
</UL>
</b>

<a name=started><HR ALIGN="right" WIDTH="85%"><FONT
SIZE="+3">G</FONT><FONT SIZE="+1">etting </FONT> <FONT
SIZE="+3">S</FONT><FONT SIZE="+1">tarted...</FONT><P></a>

To get around, just single-click on any blue or purple word or phrase
```

OK

1. Click Go, and then click View History.

2. Double-click on the line representing the Netscape opening page.

3. Click View, and then click Source.

All those lines are special commands used to design any home page and are really not that complicated. Study these lines and compare them with Figure 3.1. You'll see how the screen elements (such as the image of the dragon) correspond to specific commands such as

```
IMG SRC="images/mozwelcome.gif"WIDTH=472 HEIGHT=137 ALT=""><P>
```

This command produces the image that appears in the home page.

The Go Menu: Tracing Your Activity

Using the **Go menu**, you can bring back the previous page in the history list, go forward to the next page in the history list, use Home to go to the Netscape home page, stop the loading of a home page, and examine the history of all the home pages that have appeared in this Netscape session. You can also select a location at the bottom of the Go menu. For example, to return to the Library of Congress home page, select it from the history list you see in Figure 3.11.

FIGURE 3.11

Using the Go menu to return to a previously selected home page.

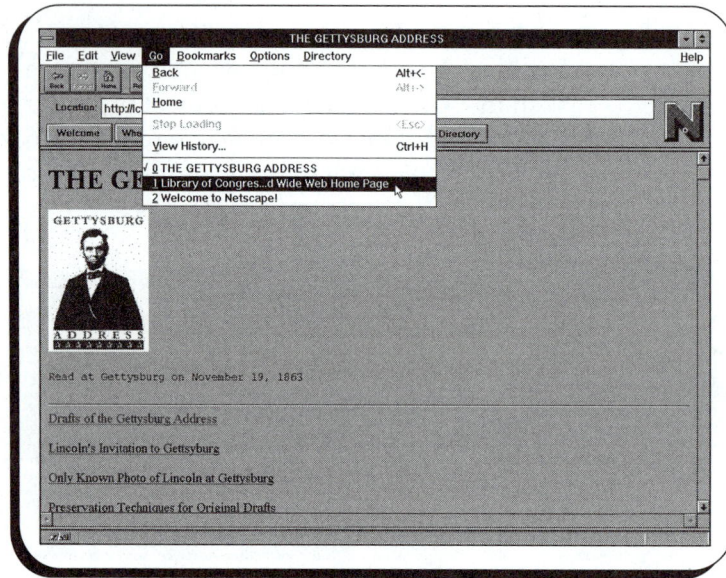

The Bookmark Menu: Keeping Track of Home Pages

We covered what the Bookmark menu offers and encourage you to take advantage of adding often-visited home pages to the list so that you can easily return when needed. Keep in mind that it is very easy to just click from here to there and from there to here and find yourself on a wonderful home page. Then you click somewhere else and can't remember how you found the underground guide to rock music home page. If you had created a bookmark, you could return there in seconds. Otherwise, you may never be able to return.

The Options Menu: Working with Netscape Options

The **Options menu** allows you to adjust many of Netscape's features or preferences. You can configure Netscape to show the Netscape Toolbar, turn the location (URL) off and on, show the directory buttons (such as What's Cool and Questions), display the security bar at the top of the Netscape Window, load images automatically, and show information received through ftp (see Chapter 5). You can also save any changes you made to the preferences and find out about other features at any time.

The Directory Menu: Exploring Netscape Directories

The final menu we'll talk about provides you with the kind of information you've probably been waiting patiently for. You can view a welcome message, learn what's new about Netscape, check out some interesting Netscape pages (What's Cool!), or go to a newsgroup (see Chapter 6). You can consult a master directory of Internet directories, search through the Internet for information, use the **Internet White Pages** to locate someone on the Internet, find out more about the Internet, and then read about Netscape Communications Corporation—the smart people who brought you Netscape.

For example, you might want to use the Internet directory to search for the name of someone you would like to locate. To begin your search, do this:

Click Directory, and then click Internet White Pages.

On this page, there is a variety of resources you can consult to try and find someone's e-mail address. As with other home pages, click on the item that interests you and follow the directions. (Notice that some of the options on the Directory menu are also shown as buttons across the top of the content area in any home page.)

FIGURE 3.12

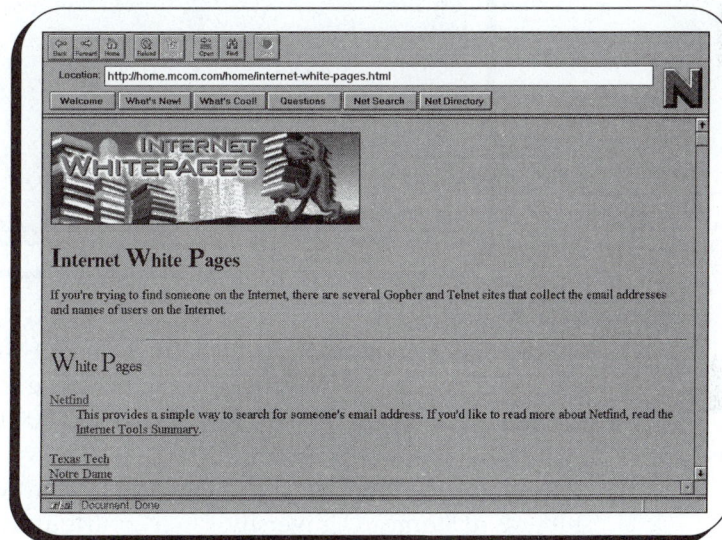

EXPLORING THE WEB

If you're even a little bit of a Web fan, read this section of the chapter with caution—or find someone else to do your homework, take over your job, and carry out your chores and other obligations. Once you get connected and start exploring, you'll find it very easy to spend hour after hour on the Web. The best way to get started is through special sites (e.g., Yahoo)—sites that give you access to Web servers (containing access to thousands of home pages) .

Yahoo at Stanford University

You have already learned how to create bookmarks of interesting places you would like to visit again. **Yahoo** is one of them and might be your first bookmark. To get to Yahoo, follow the instructions provided earlier in this chapter for locating any home page using a new URL.

1. Using regular windows procedures, highlight [the home page address] in the Location: text box.

2. Type http://akebono.stanford.edu/yahoo and press Enter. When you do this, you will see the Yahoo home page as shown in Figure 3.13.

FIGURE 3.13

The Yahoo home page.

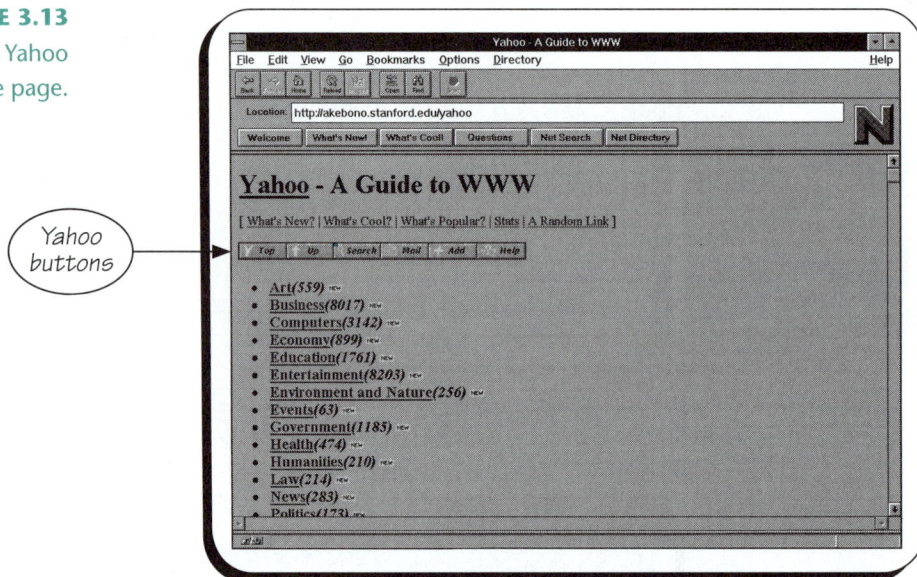

Yahoo buttons

You may not be swept off your feet by the beauty of this page, but appearances are not indicators of treasure. This home page is full of terrific links to other resources. Widely used, there are around 500,000 inquiries or hits to Yahoo hits each day.

Yahoo was stared by David File and Jerry Yang, two clever and competent students at Stanford University. Their contribution of this useful tool illustrates the spirit of the Internet and the Web. They created this home page to benefit the Web and the Net and because they wanted to share their knowledge and skills. When you gain skill and knowledge, you can contribute too.

As you can see in Figure 3.13, Yahoo is organized by a listing of topics followed by numbers. Each number indicates the number of links to that topic. As you can see, there are a ton of places to go to from here. For example, Health has 474 links with more being added every day. By clicking on any link, you go to that section. If we click on health, you will see the Yahoo page as shown in Figure 3.14.

FIGURE 3.14

The Health page
from Yahoo.

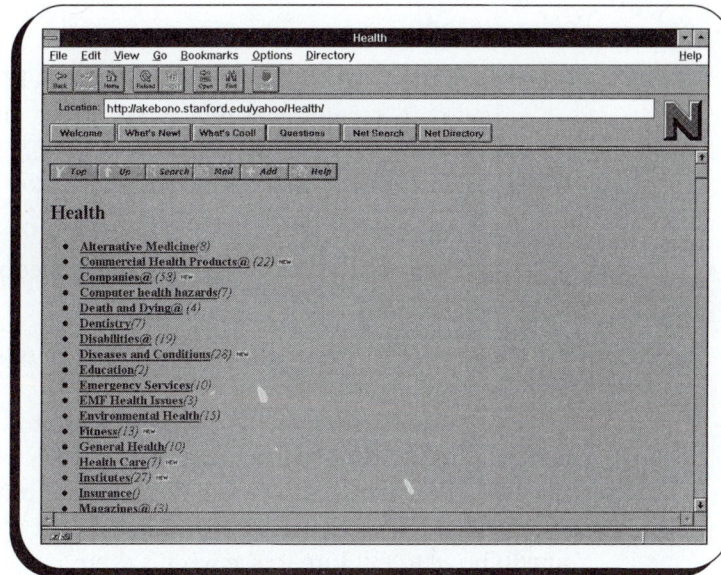

Then you can continue to click through topics until you get to the information you want and need. Starting from Yahoo, we clicked Health → Rural
Health → RuralNet and ended up at the Marshall University School of Medicine Web site as shown in Figure 3.15. You can now click on any of the selec-
tions on this home page and continue your hunt for information. Given all
you can do, now do you know why it's called Yahoo?

FIGURE 3.15

The RuralNet
home page.

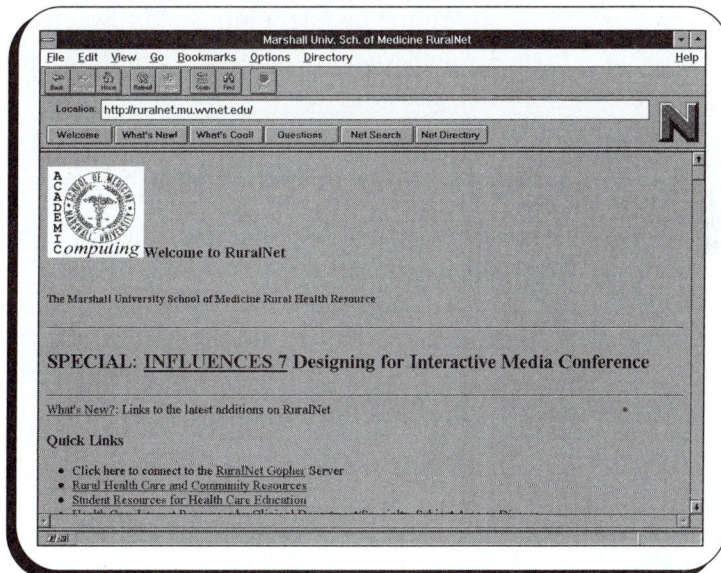

Yahoo Buttons

At the top of the Yahoo home page in Figure 3.13, you can see buttons named `What's New`, `What's Cool`, `What's Popular`, `Stats`, and `A Random Link`.

What's New is what has been added to Yahoo in the last five days.

What's Popular are the 50 most popular connections made in the past week.

What's Cool are the URLs that the Yahoo people think are cool!

Stats shows how often Yahoo is used.

A Random Link connects you at random to a link in the Yahoo database.

These buttons will provide you with links to what the Yahoo folks think is cool and popular and to the number of people who access Yahoo (Stats) daily or weekly. For example, click the What's Cool button and you'll find contests, the cool site of the day, Valentine's Day links (if it's February 14) and lots more. You will have to explore to see what's there.

There are more buttons on the home page right under What's New. These are `Top`, `Up`, `Search`, `Mail`, `Add`, and `Help`.

Top takes you to the top level of the hierarchy of pages.

Up moves you up in the hierarchy of pages.

Search allows you to search for filenames, comments, and even titles of URLs.

Add provides you with a form you can use to add a URL to Yahoo's hot list of URLs. (No guarantee that it will be added, but if you find a neat URL, the Yahoo people might seriously consider adding it.)

Help provides you with a list of questions and answers and good information about Yahoo.

Surfing the Web: A List of Web Servers

A Web server allows you to access different home pages at thousands of sites. The best place to start is

`http://www.w3.org/hypertext/DataSources/WWW/Servers.html`

as shown in Figure 3.16.

FIGURE 3.16

A summary of WWW servers organized by country.

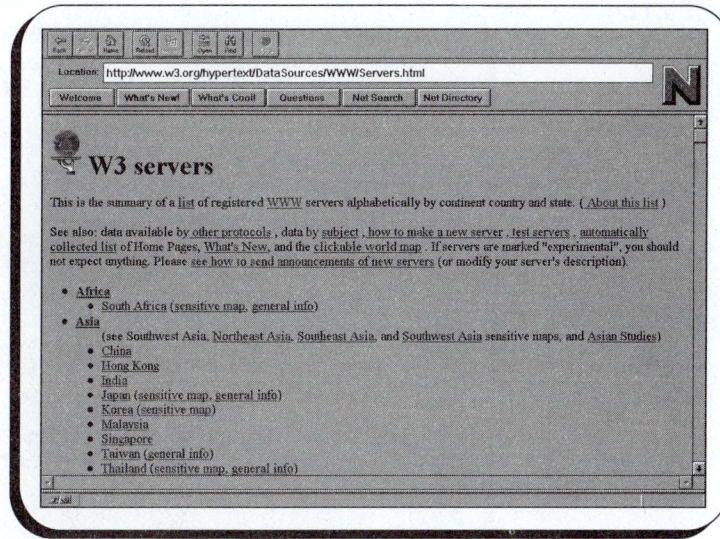

As you can see, the list is organized by country, and you can click your way to find a server at any location where you might get information. For example, let's say you have a friend who teaches at the University of Maryland and want to see if your friend has an e-mail address. Here's how you would do it.

1. From the WWW home page you see in Figure 3.16, scroll down until you see the Maryland link and click on that. You will be taken to the List of Servers (USA–Maryland) home page:

   (http://www.fie.com/www/ maryland.htm).

2. Scroll down until you get to The University of Maryland link and click. You will be taken to the University of Maryland home page:

   (http://www.umd.edu/).

3. Click University of Maryland at College Park. You will be taken to the University of Maryland at College Oark home page:

   (http://www.umcp.umd.edu/).

4. Click Who's Who (Faculty and Staff) at College Park. You will be taken to the Faculty/Staff Lookup:

   (http://inform.umd.edu/cgi-bin/phf).

   You can see what this looks like in Figure 3.17.

FIGURE 3.17

The Lookup window
at the University
of Maryland.

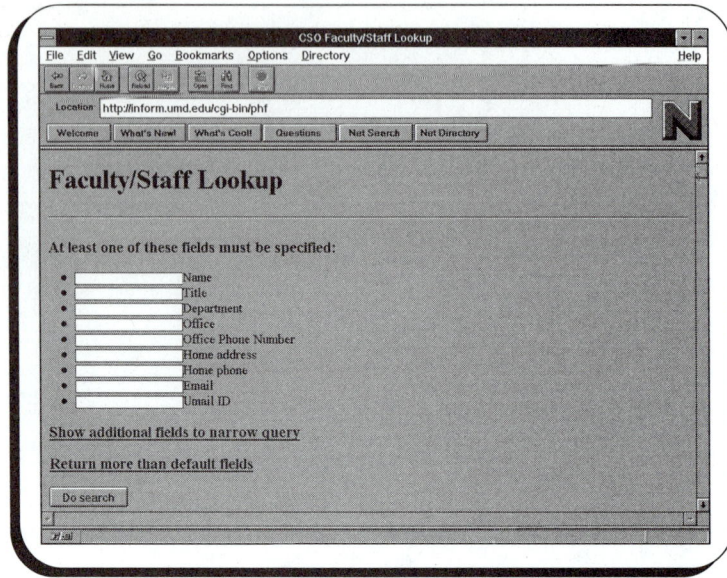

FIGURE 3.17

The Lookup window
at the University
of Maryland.

5. Fill in as much information as you can. In this example, we are looking for John Eliot and will fill in the Name space with that information.

6. Click Do Search. You can see the results of the search in Figure 3.18. There's John's name, address, phone number, and e-mail address. Success!

FIGURE 3.18

Finding an
e-mail address
using the Web.

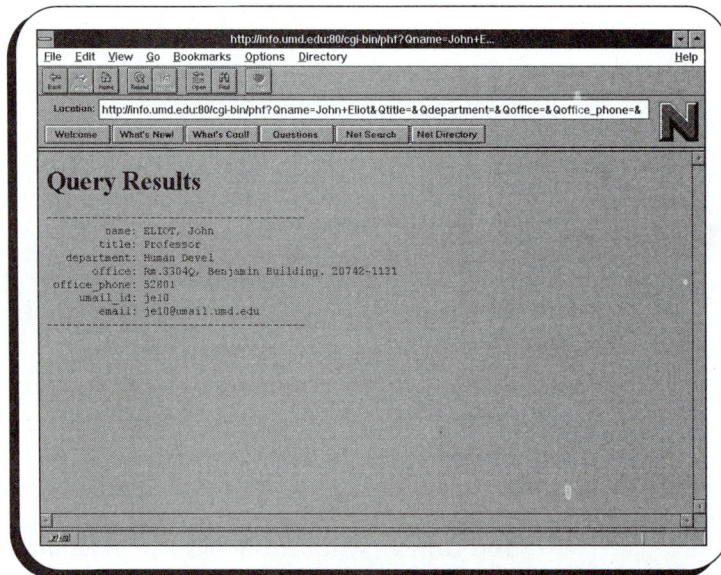

Using a Web list like the one you see in Figure 3.16 does not limit you to finding e-mail addresses. There is a ton of information on everything from The Delphi experiment at CERN, Switzerland (`http://delonline.cern.ch/delphi$ www/public/delphi/delphi.html`), which focuses on particle acceleration, to an address in Columbia, South America, with job openings at the Universidad de Los Andes (`http://www.uniandes.edu.co/`).

URouLette at the University of Kansas

Want to gamble and lose nothing and the only risk is having fun? Try this URL:

```
http://kuhttp.cc.ukans.edu/cwis/organizations/kucia/uroulette/
uroulette.html
```

and click on the roulette wheel you see in Figure 3.19. URouLette will take you, at random, to another home page on the WWW. You have no idea where you will end up, so be ready for some surprises. Remember that you can click the Back button on the Netscape Toolbar any time and be back where you started.

FIGURE 3.19
The Wheel of
Web fortune.

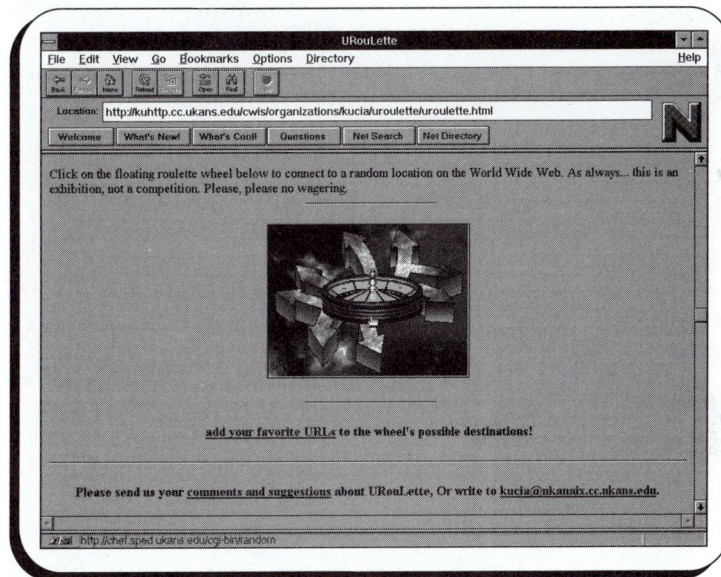

A word of warning. There's lots of neat stuff on the Web, but be aware that some of it is R-, X-, or even XXX-rated; you might inadvertently end up there if you spin the URL wheel of chance. If you're sensitive to adult-oriented text and pictures, don't fly around at random since you might find yourself somewhere you would rather not be. Better to stay away from URouLette in this case.

Ten Terrific Web Sites

You can spend hours, days, and weeks on the Web going from one location to another and seeing what each has to offer. We'll try and cut that time down for you and suggest sites that we think deserve your attention. Remember, watch your typing since URLs must be typed *exactly* as you see them here.

1. A Virtual Library (WWW Virtual Library home page)

   `http://info.cern.ch/hypertext/DataSources/bySubject/Overview.html`

   Virtual means it's not really there, but you have access to it nonetheless. The WWW Virtual Library should be your first stop while browsing the Web. Here, you can go to categories such as archaeology, electronic journals, medicine, paranormal phenomena, and hundreds more. This catalog of thousands of subjects and links is a treasure chest of information.

2. Visit the Louvre (The Louvre home page)

   `http://mistral.enst.fr/~pioch/Louvre`

   The Louvre, located in downtown Paris, is the most famous art museum in the world and the home of priceless treasures. You can not only view the permament collection but you can see current shows as well. Happy browsing.

3. Maps and More (Map Viewer home page)

   `http://pubweb.parc.xerox.com/map/`

   This is an incredible assortment and collection of maps you access with a click of the mouse. You can enter a search term or browse visually.

4. Free Stuff (Windows Shareware Archive home page)

   `http://coyote.csum.edu/cwis/winword/winword.html`

   Here's enough Windows shareware to last you for at least the next ten years. If you don't know what a selection is, shareware allows you to try it. If you like it, the understanding is that you will pay the registration fee. If you don't like it, don't use it.

5. Seek and Ye Shall Find (Search the Web home page)

   `http://webcrawler.cs.washington.edu/WebCrawler/WebQuery.html`

   The WebCrawler allows you to search through thousands of documents on the Internet using search words. It's a great place to start should you want to begin a search on almost any topic. For example, if you want to find out about Hampshire College in Amherst, Massachusetts, enter those search words and you'll be taken to a list of possible links, including the one to Hampshire College's home page.

6. Bull or Bear (QuoteCom home page)

   `http://www.quote.com`

   If you want to know what your portfolio of stocks is worth, check out QuoteCom, a service that provides end-of-day quotes, news about companies, and even information on foreign stock activity. You can try QuoteCom for free and see what it's like. If you want the service on a regular basis, you may have to pay, but it's not exactly clear what kind of arrangement is made between server and provider from the home page.

7. All You Need To Know (AskERIC Virtual Library home page)

   `http://eryx.syr.edu/COWSHome.html`

   If you ever need a reference on a particular topic in the social or behavioral sciences, or want to know what the acronym (CRTIC) stands for, or read *Moby Dick*, this is the site for you. It's a collection of educational materials and databases.

8. A Bit Different (Where the Buffalo Roam home page)

   `http://xor.com:80/wtbr/`

   Not everything on the Net is for everyone. This home page, called Where the Buffalo Roam, is a collection of cartoons that are just a bit off center (both left and right).

9. All the People, All the Time (The Constitution of the United States home page)

   `http://www.law.cornell.edu/constitution/constitution.`
   `over view.html`

   It's outlasted its harshest critics and, as we write this, it's under attack once again with the proposed addition of amendments. The Constitution of the United States home page brings you the details of history up close. Want great trivia? Look up the names of the signers of the Constitution.

10. More Really Free Stuff (Free Stuff from the Internet home page)

    `http://power.globalnews.com/articles/txt/freestuf/contents.htm`

    Here's more free stuff. You can find a ton of things to send for, most of which are free or require only a small fee for postage and handling. Visit galleries, download graphics, and read newsletters—you'll only be getting started.

There you have our ten great Web sites; however, this next one is so much fun, we couldn't resist adding an eleventh.

11. What's at the Movies (Cardiff's Movie Database Browser)

`http://www.cm.cf.ac.uk/Movies/`

Want to know what the critics thought of *The Silence of the Lambs* (Boo!)? How about *The Maltese Falcon*? How about any of some 30,000 other entries? You can get to them all through this gateway to the rec.arts. movies newsgroup (see Chapter 6) and also find out which celebs were born today (or any day), the current Academy Awards nominees, and some gossip about famous marriages. This volunteer effort is in the best spirit of the Web—informative and fun.

CREATING A HOME PAGE

Throughout this chapter, you've seen a few home pages, most of which are designed to be highly functional, easy to understand, and easy to use. Although creating a home page might seem like a mystery or a small miracle, you'll be surprised how easy it really is.

HYPERTEXT MARKUP LANGUAGE OR HTML: THE LANGUAGE OF HOME PAGES

Home pages can be simple or complex, depending upon the degree of complexity you need to get the job done. All home pages, however, are governed by the same rules which are summarized below.

- They are all written in **HTML** language. This language included commands such as <title>, <h1>, and <image>, which are almost self-explanatory. HTML resembles the codes that publishers used to insert in manuscripts before they were sent to the printer, such as <I> for italic or <b> for bold.

- HTML files are created using a word processor (and saving it as an ASCII file) or a special tool such as HTML Assistant. These files are then transferred to the computer that is your Internet connection.

- Any HTML file that you want to set up as a home page must be given public permission (from your system administrator) so that others can access it from a remote setting. After all, what sense would it make to have a home page that no one can access?

- Creating a home page in HTML is a process of trial and error. After you finish creating the home page, use your viewer (such as Netscape) to examine it before you upload it to your Internet connection. Many HTML tools, such as HTML Assistant, allow you to view your home page as it is being created. You can also open the HTML file (use the File and Open commands in Netscape) and view what the home page looks like as it is being produced. Your best bet? Go to

`http://www.ncsa.uiuc.edu/General/Internet/WWW/HTMLPrimer.html`

to get a readable and useful beginner's guide to HTML.

In Figure 3.20, you can see a simple home page that demonstrates some HTML language.

FIGURE 3.20

A simple HTML page.

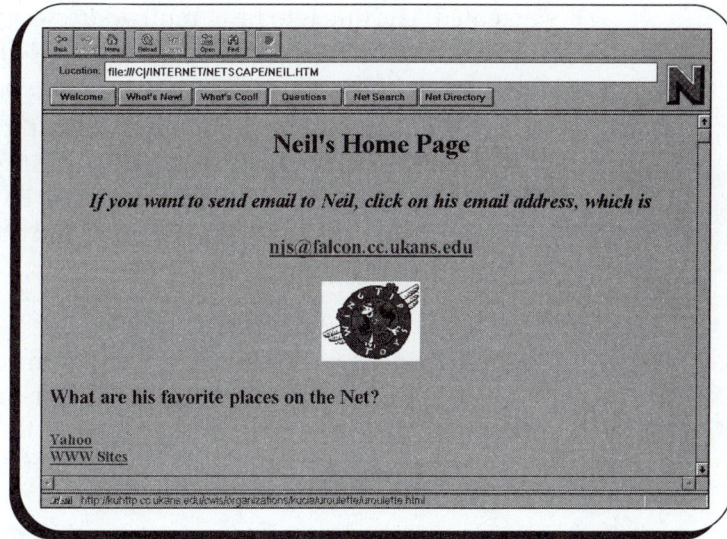

In Figure 3.21, you can see the HTML commands that were used to create this home page.

FIGURE 3.21

HTML commands used to create the home page you see in Figure 3.20

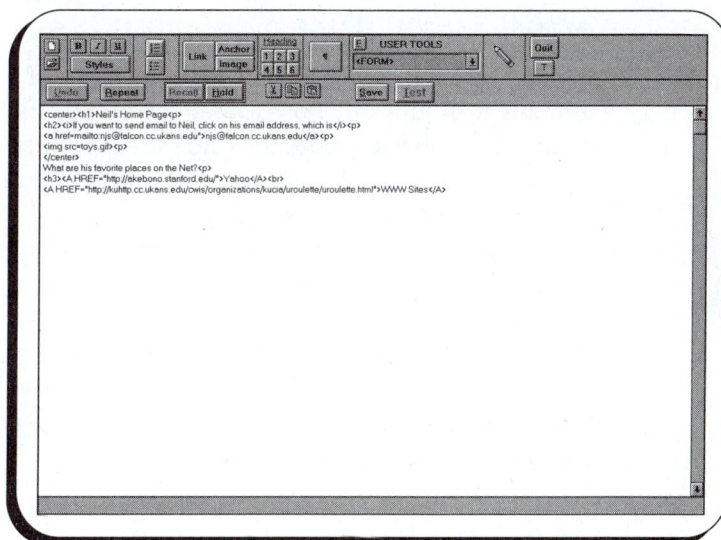

We used the HTML Assistant shown in Figure 3.21 to create this HTML file.

- Line 1 centers and enters the text, Neil's Home Page. The <h1> means a heading of size 1. You can have headings from size 1 through size 6. The <p> command is for paragraph.

- Line 2 is text that is italicized (notice the <I> command).

- In line 3, things get interesting. Here, the href stands for hypertext reference, which is what we are referring to. In other words, a link is being created. The link is to my e-mail addresse: njs@falcon.cc.uakns.edu. The end of the line could have been called Neil's e-mail address, and that's what would have appeared on the home page.

- Line 4 inserts an image to illustrate that it is easily done with the <img command. The image is in the GIF (or Graphics Interchange Format, a standard for the Net). Netscape can view BMP (bit-mapped) images, JPG (Joint Photographic Experts Group), and other formats.

- Line 5 turns centering off.

- Line 6 contains more text.

- Lines 7 and 8 create a link to Yahoo and to the location of the list of WWW sites. Once again, we pointed there using the href command and then entered the name of the site and the information we wanted to appear on the screen.

The file was then saved, transferred to the Internet connection, and given an address. How you transfer the file and what you name it depends upon your Internet provider. That's the easy part—the real challenge is to make your home page appear just the way you want it to.

A Brief Tour of HTML Assistant

It's easy and rewarding to create a home page of your own. Sometimes it's more difficult to figure out how to get the HTML file you create to your Internet connection than to create the page itself! For example, you can just highlight a line and click on the appropriate tag to enter such commands as <center> and <A HREF> on your home page.

While you can use your word processor to enter HTML commands and create a home page, there's a much easier way—using HTML Assistant or HTML Pro. Both of these programs act like HTML editors to speed up your entry of commands as well as help you design a home page with lots of neat features. There are lots of other HTML editors and, as the Web becomes more popular, there are sure to be even more. The one we're reviewing here is like Netscape— easily available and easy to use.

Where to Get HTML Assistant

You can find out where to get HTML Assistant in the list of resources in Appendix A. This is the free (and easy-to-use!) version of a much more sophisticated HTML editor called HTML Assistant Pro. Information about this product is available from Brooklyn North Software Works, 25 Doyle Street, Bedford, Nova Scotia, Canada B4A 1K4 (e-mail address is harawitz@fox.nstn.ns.ca).

KEY WORDS

bookmark
distributed hypertext documents
Edit menu
File menu
Go menu
home pages
hot links
HTML
http
Internet White Pages

Options menu
progress bar
SLIP connection
status bar
universal resource locator
URL
View menu
World Wide Web (WWW)
Yahoo

REVIEW QUESTIONS

1. What is the World Wide Web and how does it work?

2. What are some of the outstanding features of Netscape? List five things you can do in Netscape that allow you to explore the Internet.

3. What is a home page and how do you get to one? What type of language is used to create a home page?

4. Why do all home pages begin with the letters http? What is the difference between http and HTML?

5. What is the function of bookmarks in Netscape and how do you use them? Why are bookmarks useful and how do you create one?

EXPLORATION EXERCISES

1. Explain to someone who knows nothing about the Internet what the World Wide Web is and how it works. Which URL site would you take them to in order to show them how the Web works? Why?

2. Use URouLette and go to ten other home pages. What do these home pages all have in common? How do they differ from one another? Which is your favorite and why?

3. Go to the Yahoo home page and compare it with the home page image you see in Figure 3.13. How are the two different? How often do you think home pages change? What types of changes would you like to see in the current Yahoo home page?

4. If you are not already there, go to the Yahoo home page. Create a bookmark for that page. Now delete the bookmark for Yahoo. What other types of information can you obtain from the screen where you delete the bookmark? Why is that information important and how can it help you manage your Netscape activities?

5. Using the information available through the Netscape opening screen, find out what the latest release of Netscape is and where you can get it.

4

Electronic Mail for Everyone

After completing this chapter, you'll be able to

- Use Netscape to send e-mail
- Use Eudora to send mail
- Edit a Eudora mail message
- Read and reply to mail using Eudora
- Forward a Eudora mail message
- Create a signature
- Save and print mail
- Create and edit nicknames
- Personalize Eudora

In Chapter 2, we introduced you to basic Internet terms and concepts including how the Internet is accessed, what commercial Internet providers offer, and how Internet names and addresses work. In Chapter 3, you learned about Netscape and home pages and started your real tour of the Internet. Now we're ready to actually use the Internet, beginning with the feature most often used—electronic mail.

Imagine it is 1925 and you're sitting at your desk at college, writing a letter to a friend in England. You stamp the letter, mail it, and three weeks later an answer comes back. You're amazed at how fast the mail is and sit down to answer your friend's questions about how much you like college and what you'll do after you graduate.

Now imagine it's 1995 and you're writing to a friend in England. Only this time, you use **electronic mail** or **e-mail**. From your home, you compose the message, press the send key and she has it on her desk in less than 30 minutes. You're amazed that her response arrives back to you within 20 minutes. In this chapter, we'll show you how easy it is to send mail via the Internet using Netscape and Eudora. If you've never used e-mail before, you will truly be amazed.

HOW E-MAIL WORKS

E-mail works much like conventional mail. You write a message and send it to an address. The big difference is that there's no paper involved. Rather, the messages you send travel from one computer to another as fast as your voice travels in a telephone conversation—in a matter of minutes or hours rather than days or weeks.

As with conventional mail, the most important consideration is making sure the address you send the mail to is current and correct. This sometimes takes a phone call to confirm that the party you are sending mail to actually has an e-mail address. Sometimes the mail addresses mentioned in the various documents you find on the Internet are incorrect as well. When you do use an incorrect address, you'll get a message back to that effect. But just like **snail mail** (via the United States Postal Service), the message does not come back right away. It could be a few hours before you know that your mail did not go through.

For example, if you send a letter addressed to

```
Tiny Tim
Madison Square Garden
New York, New York 10022
```

it's likely to come back stamped "No Such Person At This Address" or something to that effect. But the letter wasn't rejected until it got to the post office in New York City. E-mail works in a similar way. First, the system has to try to send the message. If it is rejected by the recipient system, you will get back a message with information about the rejection which almost always says that the address is wrong. You either entered the wrong address or entered the right address incorrectly.

NETSCAPE AND E-MAIL

Although Netscape is not a mailing program, it has a limited application for e-mail: You can send mail through Netscape but not receive it. In later releases you will surely be able to send and receive mail but, until then, you will have to rely upon some other program to read your mail. We'll tell you about Eudora later in this chapter. Right now, let's see how to send mail in Netscape.

To send mail in Netscape, follow these steps.

1. Click File, and then click Mail Document. When you do this, you will see the Mail Document window as shown in Figure 4.1.
2. Click on the To box and enter [the e-mail address of the person to whom you want to send the message].

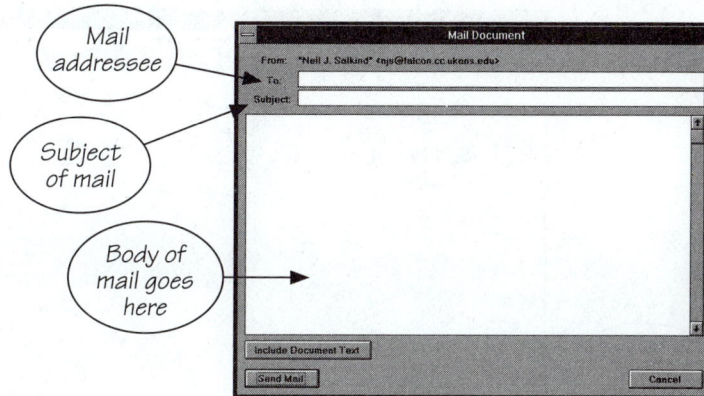

FIGURE 4.1
The Netscape Mail
Document window.

3. Press Tab twice to move to the message area.

4. Enter [the message you want to send].

5. Click Send Mail. The message will be sent to the e-mail addressee.

Since Netscape is a Windows application, you can cut, copy, and paste any information you want in the Mail Document window. Once the mail is sent, you are returned to the Netscape home page you were on when you selected the Mail Document option on the File menu.

EUDORA AND E-MAIL

While you can send mail using Netscape, it takes a fully featured mail program like **Eudora** to really manage all your mail activities. We focus on Eudora for two reasons. First, it is an easy-to-use Windows-based **mailer**. It even has simple icons that let you perform operations with a click. Second, Eudora is probably available on more systems than any other mailer. It is in use at thousands of sites and has tens of thousands of users. (I found all this out by e-mailing the developers of Eudora.) You can find out where to get Eudora in Appendix A.

Starting Eudora

To start Eudora, click on the Eudora icon ▦. When you first start Eudora, you may have to enter a password. It is the same password that you use for accessing your Internet connection. Type carefully when you enter it. See the section on Peronalizing Eudora in this chapter to learn how to turn off Eudora's request for your password and setting other defaults. When you open Eudora, you will see the Eudora opening screen as shown in Figure 4.2.

FIGURE 4.2

The Eudora
opening screen.

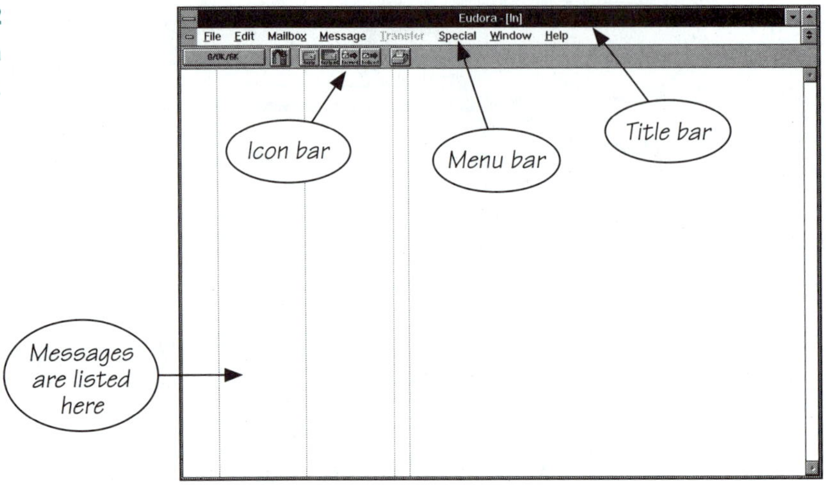

In opening a screen, you'll see any messages that are waiting for you. Since this is your first time on Eudora and your first e-mail experience, we assume that you have no messages waiting. Let's proceed then to do what one would do first—create and mail a message. If, by some chance, you do have mail waiting, you can skip to the section on how to read mail and then return here for further instructions.

The Eudora Opening Screen

Here's what you'll see in the Eudora opening screen: what each menu does and what the information in the Eudora–[In] screen represents.

- The **Title bar** indicates the current Eudora window.
- The **Menu bar** lists the eight Eudora menus that you use in creating, editing, and sending mail. We'll cover the most important of these as you work through this chapter.
- The **Icon bar** shows the icons used to delete, transfer and print mail, as well as perform other operations. Some of these icons take the place of commands located on the various menus right above the icon bar. The set of three numbers on the icon bar (1/0k/0k in Figure 4.2) indicates three things: the number of waiting messages, the size of all the messages, and the amount of unused space in the mailbox. In this example, there is one message waiting, which takes up almost zero space and zero space is wasted.
- The **Message list** indicates who sent the message, the time it was received, its size, and its subject.

Sending Mail

The best way to learn how to use Eudora, as with any tool, is by using it. For your first task, let's send a letter to President Bill Clinton. The White House runs a sophisticated e-mail service and you're sure to get an automatic response within minutes or certainly less than one hour.

To send mail using Eudora, follow these steps.

1. Click Message, and then click New Message. Figure 4.3 shows the window where you type your message. As you can see, the title is Eudora–[No Recipient, No Subject] since you have not yet designated a title or a subject. This window is called the Outgoing Message window.

FIGURE 4.3

Creating a
new message.

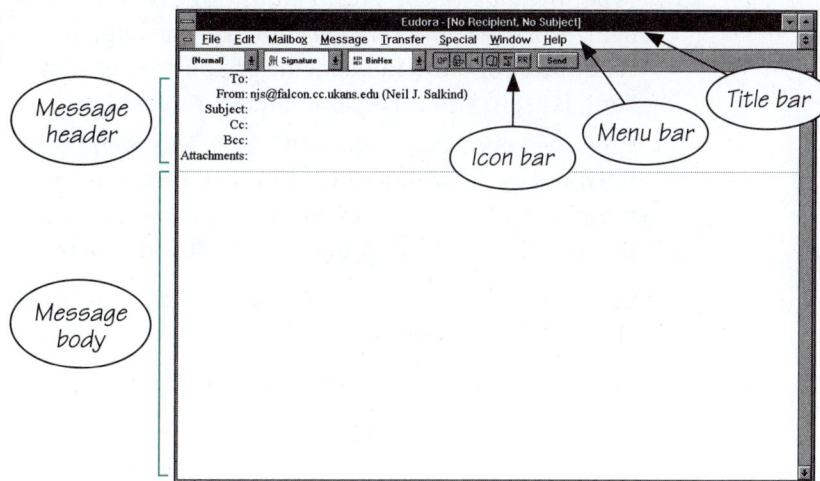

The Outgoing Message window consists of four areas.

- The title bar gives the title of the message and specifies to whom it is being sent.
- The icon bar consists of a set of icons that perform specific mail tasks.
- The **message header** contains information such as who is receiving the message, who is sending the message, the subject of the message, and various options for copying the message and attaching files.
- The message body contains the body of the message.

2. In the To: area, type president@whitehouse.gov. This is Bill Clinton's complete e-mail address. There are several header fields which allow additional information to be added to a mail message. These are Subject, Cc:, Bcc:, and Attachments:

- The Subject: field is used to define the subject of the message. Always include a message. It's e-mail etiquette to do so.
- The Cc: field (which stands for carbon copy) is used to send a copy of the message to another mail address.
- The Bcc: field (which stands for blind carbon copy) is used to send a copy of the message to another mail address, but, unlike Cc:, the addressee to whom the mail is being sent doesn't appear.
- The Attachments: field allows you to specify the location of a file and filename so that it can be attached to the e-mail message you are sending.

3. Press Tab. You will be in the subject field.

4. Type Message to the President and press Tab. You will move to the Cc: field. You are now going to copy this message to a classmate. Have the classmate copy the message he or she creates and e-mail it to the President. Be sure you have your classmate's address.

5. Type [a classmate's e-mail address]. This is the e-mail address to whom the message to President Clinton will be copied. Be sure you use a classmate's e-mail address. If you want to copy the message to more than one person, place a comma between addresses, such as

```
Cc:kdayton@falcon.cc.ukans.edu, lmargolis@unc.edu,
rhaskins@whitehouse.gov
```

6. Press Tab, and then press Tab again to move into the message area.

7. In the message area, type

Dear President Clinton:
     As you can see, I am learninghow to send electronic mail over the Internet. I thought it would be fun too e-mail you a short note and see what typ of response I get back. Good luck in your work.

Neil J. Salkind

Type the message exactly as you see it above, errors and all. Be sure to substitute your name at the end of the message for the name used in the example. There are three mistakes in this note; *learninghow* (no space), *too* (should be to), and *typ* (should be type). We'll correct them all before we send the message. The composed mail message is shown in Figure 4.4.

FIGURE 4.4

A Eudora mail message to the President.

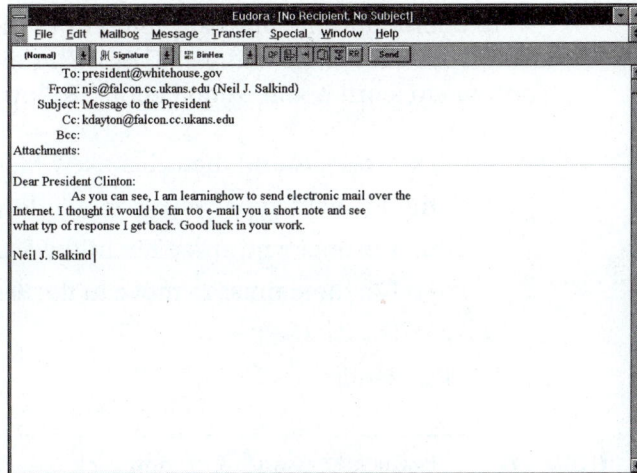

Editing a Mail Message

Eudora is such a well-designed program that surely a new release will have a spell checker just as the best word processors do. But for now, since Eudora does not have a spell checker, we'll have to do the editing the old-fashioned way. Follow these steps to edit the message to the President.

1. Click the mouse pointer between the g and the h in learning how, and then press the spacebar once.
2. Double-click on the word too, and then type to.
3. Place the mouse pointer after the letter p in the word typ and then type e. The corrected text should appear as follows.

```
Dear President Clinton:
     As you can see, I am learning how to send electronic mail
over the Internet. I thought it would be fun to e-mail you a
short note and see what type of response I get back. Good luck
in your work.

Neil J. Salkind
```

Once the spelling is checked and you are sure you want to send the message, click the Send button. Remember that once you click **Send**, the message is gone. There's no changing your mind and going to the mailbox to take the letter out and rewrite it. Messages that are sent are automatically saved in the Out Mailbox. If you want to see a list of these messages, select Out from the **Mailbox menu**. You can select any message to examine and mail again, but you cannot edit the content of the message. If you want to revise the message, select the entire message and paste it into a new message window. Only then can you edit it.

In addition to the message you sent to the President, send one to yourself using your own mail address. This is the message you will reply to as you continue to learn about using Eudora. Follow these steps:

1. Click Message, and then click New Message.
2. In the To: field, type [your e-mail address].
3. Press Tab once and enter Test in the Subject: field.
4. Press Tab three times to move to the Message field.
5. Type This is a test.
6. Click Send.

HOW TO SEND MAIL IN EUDORA

1. Click Message, and then click New Message.
2. Enter a complete e-mail address and a Subject message.
3. Enter the message you want to send.
4. Click Send.

More About the Outgoing Message Window

You clicked on the Send button to send the mail, but as you can see in Figure 4.5, there are several other icons on the icon bar that you could have clicked.

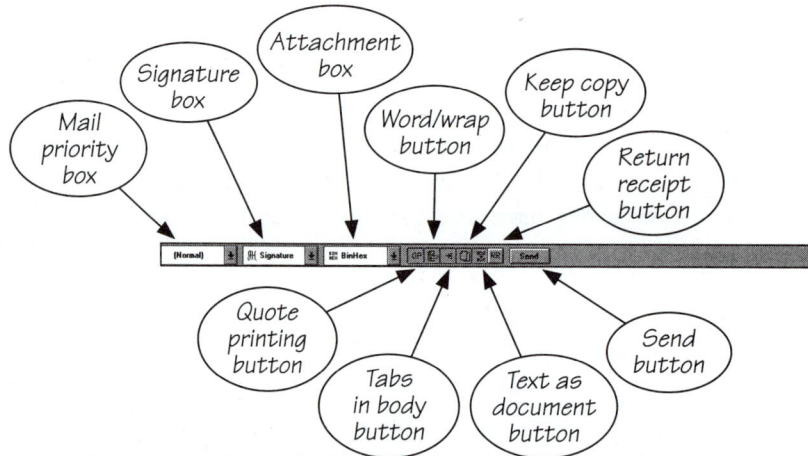

FIGURE 4.5
The Outgoing Message icon bar.

- The **mail priority box** allows you to set a priority for your message. For example, you may have a series of messages to send and you want one of them sent first. You would assign it the highest priority.
- The **signature box** allows you to attach a signature or a fixed ending to a message.

- The **attachment combo box** allows you to select the format of the files you are going to attach to the mail message. You are best to stick with ASCII or text files, represented by the BinHex option on this box.

- The **quote printing box button** allows you to send long lines of special characters.

- The **word wrap button**, when on, causes Eudora not to require a carriage return when entering text. Like a word processor, this means that words will not break in the middle of a word at the end of a line but rather wrap around to the next line.

- The **tabs in body button** results in Eudora entering the spaces to the next tab stop.

- The **keep copy button** automatically files a copy of the message in the Out mailbox. The copy is kept there until it is deleted.

- The **text as document button** will send attachments to the message as separate text files rather than as part of the original message.

- The **return receipt button** lets you know that your mail message has been received. This receipt is placed in your mailbox.

- The **send button** sends the active message.

Reading and Replying to Mail

As you can see in Figure 4.6, our message to the President has been received and answered. Also, you can see the e-mail message you sent to yourself (your name should appear). If you were working in Eudora when the mail was received, you might have seen a visual prompt on the screen or heard an audio prompt informing you of new mail. If you are working at a busy time of day, it may take more time for the President's mail server to respond. If a dot (•) appears next to the message, it indicates that the message has not been read yet.

FIGURE 4.6

The In window with the President's replay noted.

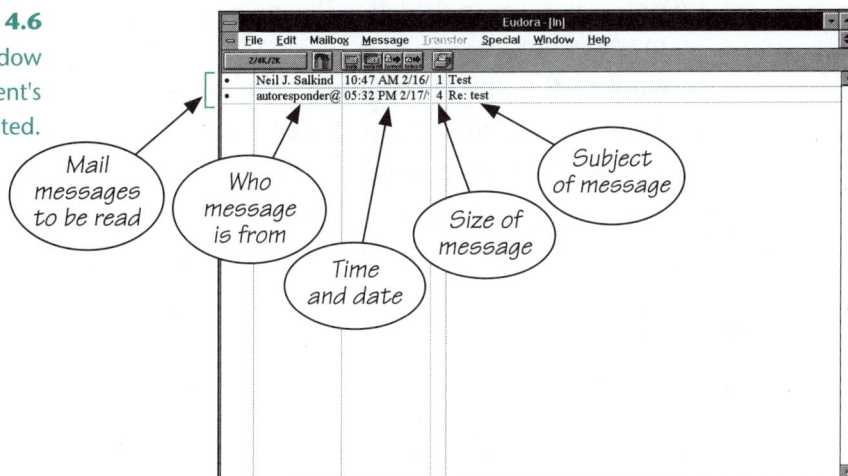

Here's what the different elements are in the In window or **mailbox** you see in Figure 4.6. As with the Message window, there's a title bar that indicates the current window and an icon bar. The icon bar contains icons that perform the following functions.

- The mailbox size button tells you the number of messages in the mailbox; the size is the total amount of disk space those messages take up; and the third number is the amount of unused disk space in the mailbox.
- The trash button deletes the highlighted message.
- The reply button produces a reply to a highlighted message. Click this when you want to respond.
- The reply all button generates a reply to each highlighted message in the mailbox.
- The forward button forwards a message to another recipient.
- The redirect button will send a message to someone you think is more appropriate to receive the message than you. When you forward a message, it goes from you to the person to whom you are forwarding it. When you redirect a message, it appears to go directly from the person who originally mailed it to the person you are forwarding it to.
- The print button prints the selected message(s). A message does not have to be open for you to print it. If you want to print more than one message at a time, hold the Shift key down as you click on each message so that more than one is selected. Then you can print all the selected messages.

In the first column, next to each message, is an indicator of the message status. Here's what the various marks and characters mean.

A • means that the message is new and has not been read.

A blank or nothing to the left of the message sender's name means that the message has been read.

An R means that the message has been replied to.

An F means that the message has been forwarded.

An S means that the message has been sent.

A - means that the message was transferred from the Out mailbox (which keeps a record of all messages sent) before it was sent.

Reading Mail

Reading mail is as easy as double-clicking on the message you want to read. In Figure 4.7, you can see the results of double-clicking on the message that was received from the President. To read mail, follow these steps:

FIGURE 4.7

The message from
the president's
office.

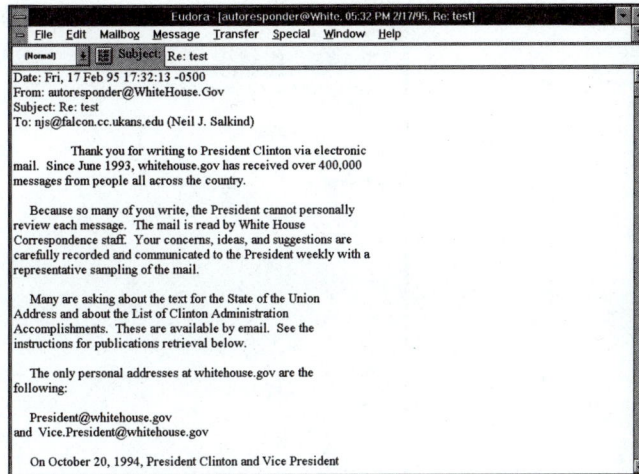

1. Double-click on [the message you want to read].
2. Scroll through the message and read it.

When you read through the message from the President's office, you will discover that he does not want you to reply to his message—it would create too much mail. Instead, there are instructions explaining how to send other messages to the White House. You might also want to explore the White House's WWW page mentioned on the second page of his reply. To close the message from the White House, click File, then click Close, or use the Ctrl+W key combination.

Replying To Mail

You still have two messages waiting for you: one that you have written to yourself and one from the President's e-mail address. Let's reply to the message that you sent yourself. To reply to a message, follow these steps. You should be in the In window.

1. Double-click on the message named Test. You should see the content of the message that you sent to yourself.
2. Click Message, and then click Reply, or use the Ctrl+R key combination. When you do this, you will see the Reply screen as shown in Figure 4.8. The To:, From:, and Subject: lines are already complete and the content of the original message is shown as well (with each line preceded by a >). As you can see, the address of the person who sent you the message is automatically entered in the To: line since this is a response to his or her message.

FIGURE 4.8

The Eudora
Reply screen.

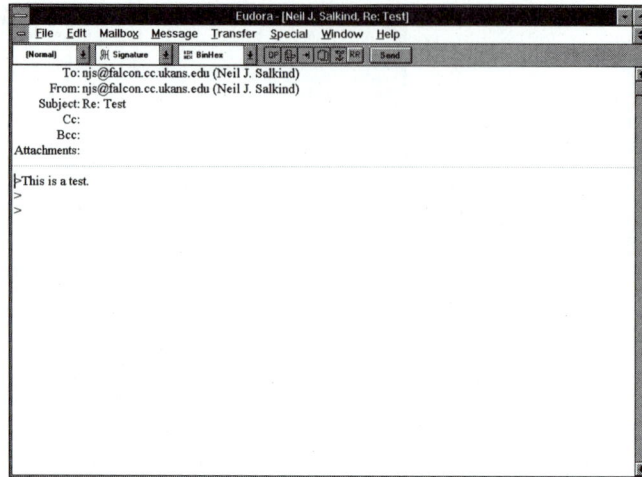

3. Press Enter once and the ↑ so you have a clear line to type. Or, if you pre-fer, use standard Window's cut procedures to delete any or all of the original text. Some people like to have the original text on the screen when they write a response and some people do not.

4. Type This is a response to your message.

5. Click Send. The mail will be sent to the address in the To: location.

Forwarding a Message

There are times you will receive mail that you know will be of particular inter-est to other parties. For example, plans for when and where your study group is meeting would be worth passing on. In this event, you will want to forward the mail to another party who may not have received the original message. To forward mail, follow these steps.

1. Select or open the message you want to forward.

2. Click Message, and then click Forward. You'll see a window very similar to the standard reply window, except that each line of the message has >> before it rather than >. This reminds the sender that the message is being forwarded.

Creating a Signature

You might have seen mail that has a unique ending to it. For example, some people create their own small designs using characters, messages, and so forth that appear at the end of any mail they send. This is their **signature** and is attached automatically. This is done by creating a file using the Signature option on the Window menu and saving it. Then any outgoing mail will be accompanied by this signature. Here's how the following signature was created and automatically attached to the mail you see in Figure 4.9.

```
---------------------------------
-"It ain't over till it's over."-
-                     Yogi Berra-
---------------------------------
```

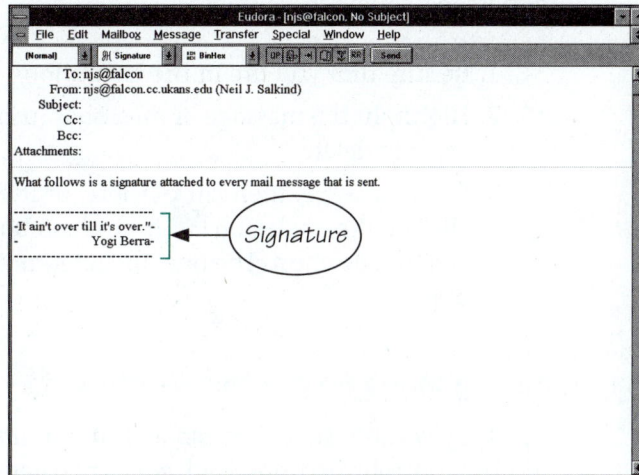

1. Click Window, and then click Signature.
2. Create the signature you want to appear at the end of each mail message. It can consist of a quotation that describes you, your name and e-mail address, or any text. A signature cannot contain graphics (too bad).
3. Click File, and then click Save.

The signature will appear at the end of every document you mail. You can't edit a signature; if you want to change it, you will have to create a new one. If a signature does not appear at the end of a mail message and you are sure that you created one correctly (and saved it!), confirm that the Use Signature box in the Switches dialog box (in the composition area) is checked.

Editing or Deleting a Signature

To edit a signature, select Signature from the Window command and make whatever changes you want. Just remember to save the Signature file when you are finished. If you want to delete your signature, select everything in the open Signature file window and then press Del to delete the text. Then save the deletion. Of course, you are saving nothing in the Signature file—which is what will appear at the end of your message: nothing. Congratulations! The signature is deleted.

Deleting Mail

Deleting mail is as simple as any other Eudora operation. To delete a message, however, you must be in the mailbox window as shown in Figure 4.6. To delete a message, follow these steps.

1. Be sure that you are in the In mailbox window.
2. Highlight the message or messages (using the Shift+click operation) you want to delete.
3. Click Message, then click Delete, or use the Ctrl+D key combination, or click on the trash icon 🗑 in the icon bar. Eudora will not ask you to confirm the deletion. The one line reference to it in the mailbox will just disappear.

Saving Mail and the Out Mailbox

You may want to save a message that you have created. For example, if it's a long or complicated one and your Internet connection is prone to crashes, saving before you send can be extra insurance. Here's how to save a message:

1. Click File, and then click Save. The message is now saved in the Out mailbox, a record of all messages that have been created and saved or created and sent.

To see the messages in the Out mailbox, follow this procedure.

1. Click Mailbox, and then click Out. You will see the Out mailbox as shown in Figure 4.10. Here you can see that all the messages except the last one have been sent. Each is annotated with an S to the left of the address where the message was sent. The one message that was saved and not sent has a • to the left of the address. This means it has been saved but not sent.

FIGURE 4.10

The Out mailbox.

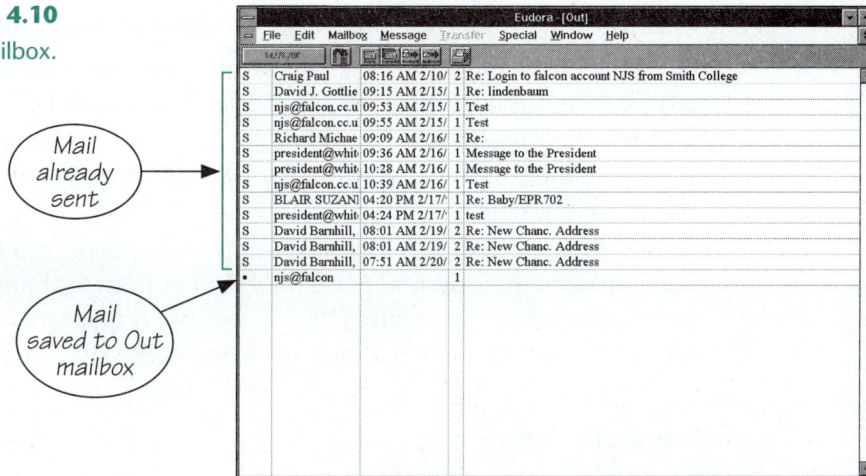

Mail already sent

Mail saved to Out mailbox

Once you have saved a message, retrieving it is simple. To retrieve a saved message, follow these steps.

1. Click Mailbox, and then click Out.
2. Double-click on the message you want to retrieve. The saved message will open in a new window. You can retrieve any message that you have sent or saved. One time-saving strategy is to retrieve a message you have already sent to someone you want to send another message to, and just change the message body since the address and other information in the headers will probably be exactly the same.

Saving Mail to a New File

If you want to save mail to a disk or some other location and not to the Out mailbox, use the Save As command on the File menu. When you select this command, the Save As dialog box will open and you will be prompted to enter a name for the file and location. The file will be saved as an ASCII or text file, which can be read by any word processor.

Mailing Other Files Using Eudora

You have learned how you can work with messages you created within Eudora. You can also mail a message in Eudora that you might have created using a word processor or some other application. If you have a letter that you created in WordPerfect for Windows or Word for Windows and want to send it but do not want to retype it, follow these directions.

1. Click File, and then click Open Text File. An Open dialog box appears.
2. Enter the name of the text file you want to import to Eudora. A text file is a file that has been saved in ASCII or text format. It has no formatting such as columns, bold, or special margins. In order to import such a file, you must first save that file using the text option on the application that was used to create it.
3. Click OK. The file (if it is in text format) will appear as a file in Eudora and you can cut, copy, and paste information from that file into the mail message you want to create. The file does not appear in a message window so it cannot be sent without first being copied to a message window.

Printing Mail

Mail that has just been created, saved, sent, retrieved, or received can be easily printed so that you can keep a hard copy—a more permanent record of your transactions. To print any document in Eudora, follow these steps.

1. Be sure the message you want to print is active and appears on your screen.
2. Click File, and then click Print. When you do this, the Print dialog box you see in Figure 4.11 will open.

FIGURE 4.11
The Print dialog box.

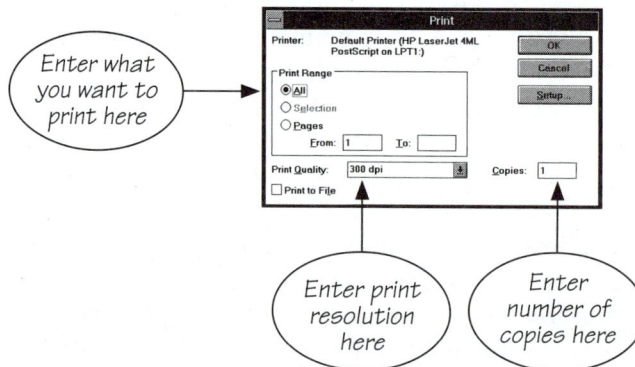

As you can see, you can print the entire document, a specific selection (that you highlight), or a range of pages. You can also change the number of copies (one copy is the default), adjust the print quality (if your printer has this capability), and even click on Print to File and save the message to a file that is stored on a disk. To change printers, click Setup and select the printer you want to use, then continue to complete the options in the Print dialog box.

You can also print any message listed in the In or Out mailbox by highlighting the message information and then selecting Print from the File menu. If you want to print more than one message, highlight more than one information line by holding down the Shift key as you click on the various messages.

CREATING NICKNAMES Wouldn't you think you would grow tired of entering lmargolis@fedora.cc.unc.edu every time you wanted to write to your friend Lew? You would. That's why Eudora, and many other mail packages, offer a simple way to enter long addresses—through the creation of a nickname. A **nickname** takes the place of someone's e-mail address. It becomes an alias (or something that stands for something else) for another person's e-mail address. For example, lmargolis@fedora.cc.unc.edu could be lew, pretsky@network.com could be phyl, and leni_sim@delphi.com could be leni.

To create a nickname for yourself, follow these steps.

1. Click Window, and then click Nickname. The Nicknames window you see in Figure 4.12 opens.

FIGURE 4.12
The Nicknames window.

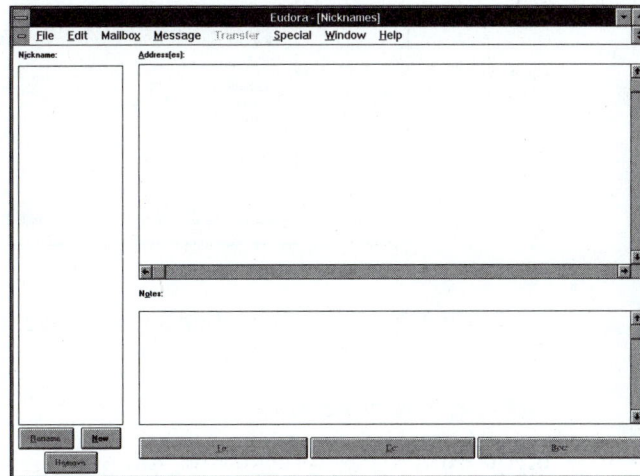

2. Click New. The New Nickname dialog box is displayed in Figure 4.13.

FIGURE 4.13
The New Nickname dialog box.

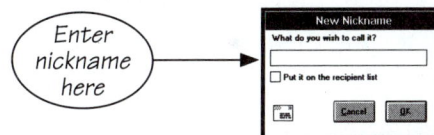

3. Type [a nickname for yourself]. You want it to be short and easy to remember. In this example, the nickname will be Neil.

4. Click the Put it on the recipient list, and then click OK. The name is added to the Nickname list in the Nicknames dialog box and the insertion point is placed in the Address(es): field. The name will then show up on the Quick Recipient list, which will become a menu item we will show you later on in this chapter.

5. Type [the complete e-mail address] of the address that corresponds with the nickname. In this example it is njs@falconm.cc.ukans.edu.

6. Click in the Notes section and add whatever other information you might like. In this case, the snail mail address for the person was added. The finished Nicknames dialog box appears in Figure 4.14.

FIGURE 4.14

The finished Nicknames dialog box.

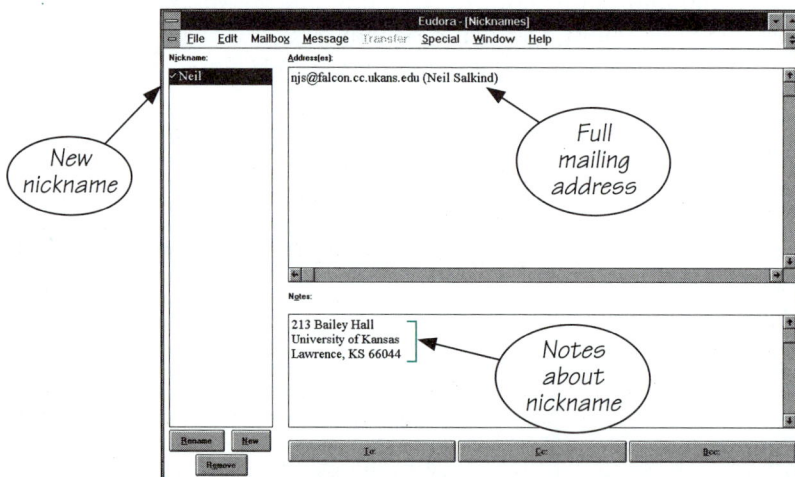

7. Click File, and then click Save to save the Nicknames you created.

Editing a Nickname

If you want to edit a nickname, follow these steps.

1. Click Window and then click Nicknames.
2. Click on [the nickname] you want to edit.
3. Click Rename and edit the nickname.
4. Click OK, and then save the Nicknames file.

Using Nicknames

All the nicknames that you create will be listed in the Nicknames file, ready to be used in a variety of ways. To use a nickname in a new message, follow these steps.

1. Click Message, and then click New Message To.
2. Select the [nickname you want to use] from the Quick Recipient list as shown in Figure 4.15.

FIGURE 4.15

Selecting a
nickname.

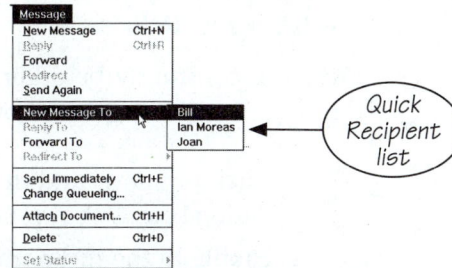

3. The complete nickname will be entered into the To: field in a new message and the e-mail address from the sender will be entered in the From: field. Now complete the Subject line, enter the body of the mail message, and send it.

You can also create a new nickname by clicking Special and then clicking Make Nickname. You'll see the New Nickname dialog box as you saw in Figure 4.13. Create the new nickname as you did before.

Another way that you can use the Nicknames feature to start a mail message is through the Nicknames dialog box. To start such a message, follow these steps:

1. Click Window, and then click Nicknames.

2. Click the nickname representing the person to whom you want to send a mail message.

3. Click To: and a new message window will appear with the nickname in the To: field and your mail address in the From: field.

Making Nicknames from Mail You Receive

This is a really fast way to make a nickname and save lots of steps, but it only works when you get mail from someone you want to create a nickname for. When a friend sends you mail, you can easily and quickly create a nickname for that friend with a few clicks, without ever having to enter his or her address. To create a nickname from a received mail message, follow these steps:

1. Open a mailbox so that you can see the mail message listed.

2. Click Special and then click Make Nickname.

3. In the New Nickname dialog box, enter the nickname you want to use, and then click OK. The nickname will be added to the Quick Recipient list. The next time you want to send that person mail, his or her nickname will be on the Quick Recipient list. It only takes two clicks (Message, New Message To..., and then the nickname) to get a mail message started.

Deleting a Nickname

You will constantly be adding and deleting nicknames as your mail habits change. You already know how to create a nickname—here's how to delete one.

1. Click Window, and then click Nicknames. You will see the Nicknames dialog box as shown in Figure 4.12.

2. Highlight the nickname you want to delete.

3. Click Remove.

4. Click File, and then click Save. Any nicknames that were deleted from the Nickname dialog box will be deleted from the file and will no longer be available on the Quick Recipient list.

Personalizing Eudora

Any Internet application that's as cool as Eudora has more tricks than you can imagine. One whole set has to do with personalizing Eudora to better fit the way that you work. Here are ten of the many things you can do to change basic Eudora features. The first seven of these changes take place in the Switches dialog box found on the Special menu you see in Figure 4.16. The last three suggestions can be addressed within the Configuration dialog box.

FIGURE 4.16

The Switches dialog box.

1. Signature or Not?

   If the Use Signature box is checked, Eudora will automatically place the signature at the end of the message.

2. Word Wrap or Not?

   If the Word Wrap box is checked, Eudora will not require a carriage return at the end of each line of type in an outgoing message. Word wrap saves you time and trouble because you don't have to worry about hyphenation and where lines end and new ones begin.

3. Want a Copy?

   If you want a copy of the messages you send to go to the Out mailbox for later reference, then check the Keep Copies box. If you don't, anything you send will then be trashed and it's bye-bye forever.

4. Be Gone, Password Prompt!

   If you never want to have to enter your password when you start Eudora, click Save Password. This means that your password is stored on your computer—not a great idea if you are concerned about security. If that's the case, better leave the Save Password box *not* checked and enter your password each time you start.

5. Sending Messages

   The Send On Check box, when checked, will send any messages that you have created and not yet sent. Eudora will send them the next time it checks your mail.

6. Incoming Mail!

   With the Alert box checked, Eudora will display a dialog box whenever new mail is received. If you want this dialog box accompanied by a cute sound, click Sound. If you want even more of a notice, click Open In Box and Eudora will open the In box when new mail arrives—almost forcing you to stop what you are doing and take notice.

7. Empty Trash

   With this option checked, Eudora empties the Trash mailbox when you quit Eudora. The Trash mailbox is where your deleted messages go. You can retrieve them if you change your mind, but you have to do it before you quit your Eudora session. If this option is not checked, the Trash mailbox will only be emptied when you select Empty Trash from the Special menu. It's a good idea not to make this option active when you first start using Eudora. Wait until you are used to the way the mail program works. Then, should you accidentally trash a message, you can always recover it from the Trash mailbox.

   Here are some other custom changes you can make in the Configurations dialog box on the Special menu as shown in Figure 4.17.

FIGURE 4.17
The Configuration
dialog box.

8. Changing Fonts

   You can change the font that is used for the on-screen appearance of mail as well as for printing mail. Just click on the Screen Font and Printer Font drop-down menus, select the type of font you want to use, and select the size.

9. Check My Mailbox, Please

   In the Configuration dialog box, you can also indicate how often you want Eudora to check your mail. In Figure 4.17, you can see that the mail is checked every 15 minutes. Along with some other of the options listed in the Switches dialog box (such as the Alert option as shown in Figure 4.16), you can work something out that suits the way you work.

10. How Big?

   You can set the number of characters in the width of a message in the `Message Width:` box. If you use a big font to create a message, a width smaller than the 80 character default might be useful.

QUITTING EUDORA

Quitting Eudora is as simple as quitting any Windows application—here's how.

Click File, and then click Exit. If you have any messages that have not been sent, Eudora will remind you of this and give you a chance to send the mail before you exit. You'll then be returned to the window containing the Eudora icon.

ADVANTAGES AND DISADVANTAGES OF E-MAIL

E-mail is fast, convenient, and, for many Internet users, cheap. It's also very reliable. If you do your job right, the likelihood of mail getting to where it should go is greater than 99 percent. On the negative side, there are some serious concerns. First, there's little privacy or security. It's pretty easy to access other people's mail, especially if you are on a commercial service. Second, e-mail is easy to falsify (just type what looks like an e-mail screen and print it out!), so it's impossible to verify that a document received via e-mail and printed out is genuine. Because of this, e-mail can't be used for business or legal transactions. They almost always need to be backed up by a printed copy.

Finally, there's no **paper trail**. What's a paper trail? It's a printed record of a series of transactions. When you send U.S. mail back and forth to a friend, you leave a paper trail. Paper trails are important for several reasons, but are most important for the historian and others interested in a record of any transaction between people or institutions. Earlier you saw how easy it is to write to the President (and anyone else for that matter) via e-mail. But no matter what transacts between you and his office, there's no hard copy record unless there are printouts of the mail. Then we're back to the previous problem. How do you verify the authenticity of the documents? These are all issues that will be addressed as e-mail becomes more popular. It will be interesting to see how creative people (such as those who serve on the IAB) approach them.

MAILING TO OTHER CONNECTIONS

Not everyone has an Internet address. However, many people who don't have addresses have connections through a **gateway** to the Internet. A gateway is a connection between two networks. It translates the mail from one system to another. What follows is a listing of other e-mail services where you are likely to find your friends or your colleagues and directions on how you can reach them using a basic Internet e-mail address. Be sure to use nicknames that you learned about so you only have to enter an address once. Some of these services will charge your friends to accept mail from outside their own network. See Table 4.1 for a list of common e-mail providers where your friends may have e-mail addresses. These e-mail providers are connected by gateways and are not the gateways themselves.

TABLE 4.1   Eudora keyboard shortcuts.

Use this key combination . . .	To . . .
[CTRL]+[A]	Select all the text in a message
[CTRL]+[C]	Copy text
[CTRL]+[D]	Delete text
[CTRL]+[E]	Send an outgoing message
[CTRL]+[F]	Open the Find window
[CTRL]+[H]	Attach a document to the outgoing message
[CTRL]+[I]	Open the In mailbox
[CTRL]+[K]	Create a nickname
[CTRL]+[L]	Open the nicknames window
[CTRL]+[M]	Check mail
[CTRL]+[N]	Create a new message
[CTRL]+[O]	Open a message
[CTRL]+[P]	Print a selected or active message
[CTRL]+[Q]	Quit Eudora
[CTRL]+[R]	Reply to a message
[CTRL]+[S]	Save the contents of the active window
[CTRL]+[V]	Paste text
[CTRL]+[W]	Close the active message
[CTRL]+[X]	Cut text
[CTRL]+[Z]	Undo

A SUMMARY OF EUDORA KEYBOARD COMMANDS

If you're not a mouser (some people like their hands to remain on the keyboard), Table 4.2 shows you a set of keyboard equivalents for the mouse moves you learned in this chapter.

TABLE 4.2 Gateways for sharing mail through the Internet.

e-Mail Service	Address Format	Example
ALANet	username%alanet-@intermail.isi.edu	njs%alanet-@intermail.isi.edu
America Online	username@aol.com	njs@aol.com
AppleLink	username@applink.apple.com	njs@applink.apple.com
ATTMail	username@attmail.com	njs@attmail.com
Bitnet	username@host.bitnet or username%host@gateway	njs@ukans.bitnet or njs@ukans.bitnet
BIX	username@bix.com	njs@bix.com
CompuServe	userid@compuserve.com	70404,365@compuserve.com
Delphi	username@delphi.com	njs@delphi.com
EcoNet	username@igc.org	njs@igc.org
Genie	username@genie.geis.com	njs@genie.geis.com
GeoNet	username:geo4@map.das.net	njs:geo4@map.das.net
MCI Mail	userid@mcimail.com	8673475@mcimail.com
Prodigy	username@prodigy.com	njs@prodigy.com
SprintMail	/G=givenname/S=surname /O=organization/ADMD=Telemail /C=US/@sprint.com	/G=neil/S=salkind/O=ku /ADMD=Telemail/C=US /@sprint.com
The Well	username@well.sf.ca.us	njs@well.sf.ca.us
UUCP	username@domain name	njs@ukans.edu

E-MAIL NETIQUETTE

Sending e-mail is not always as simple as connecting to the Net and just sending a message. There are some conventions you have to follow as far as addressing and such, and even some social ones you need to attend to as well. You can find our e-mail netiquette suggestions in Box 4.1.

BOX 4.1
Guidelines for e-mail netiquette

1. While you think that your mail is private, it may indeed not be.

2. Only send those things that you could stand everyone in the neighborhood, office, and school knowing about.

3. Once you have finished reading a message, delete it so as to keep active files to a minimum and free up space for every one.

4. Check your mail on a regular basis. It will help you keep current, have your correspondents in mind, and clear unwanted articles when you are done.

5. If you want to keep a mail message, save it to a file and then download it to your own storage facility. That saves space and costs for the system.

Here are two mail messages from troubled readers to Miss Manners (Queen of Netiquette) about the proper way to use e-mail. While these messages are meant to be humorous in nature, you'll find that the more you use mail, the more issues such as proper conduct become important.

Dear Miss Manners:

I have just connected to the Internet and sent my first e-mail message but am troubled by how I should address my party and what rules of etiquette I should follow. Please help.

On-line at egr@utg.edr.edu

Dear Gentle E-Mailer:

You are not alone. Millions of us each month are joining the Net to send mail and have the very same concerns. Perhaps you should see the sections on netiquette, and especially the one on e-mail in chapter 4. Best wishes for successful e-mailing.

missmanners@benice.com

Once you're an official e-mailer, you're really on your way to using the Internet. You can mail all over the world with a few keystrokes and receive mail back, often in only a matter of minutes. What you especially need to remember about the Eudora mail command is that typing addresses correctly is very important. Otherwise, you'll see your mail get sent and it could be hours or days before you find out that it never really got to where it was going. While e-mail is an important part of the Internet, accessing thousands of files from hundreds of different computers speaks to the true spirit of what the information superhighway is about: sharing resources. On to ftp!

KEY WORDS

attachment box
electronic mail or e-mail
Eudora
gateway
icon bar
keep copy button
mail priority box
mailbox
mailbox menu
mailer
menu bar
message header
message list

nickname
paper trail
quote printing box button
return receipt button
send
send button
signature
signature box
snail mail
tabs in body button
test as document button
title bar
word wrap button

REVIEW QUESTIONS

1. What are some of the advantages and disadvantages of e-mail? See if you can provide three personal and three professional uses for e-mail.

2. What are some of the advantages of a mailer such as Eudora over mail in Netscape?

3. In Eudora, what is the difference between the In and Out mailboxes?

4. In the In mailbox, what does a • represent? An R? A blank space?

5. How would you get help on the Save command in Eudora?

EXPLORATION EXERCISES

1. Let's say you've created an address book and have the entry

   `Harriet        Harriet Most        hm@uwm.edu`

   You enter Harrite (instead of Harriet) in the To: header and press the Enter key. What happens?

2. Send a message to the system administrator at your Internet site so that you can practice sending mail. The address is probably postmaster@[domain name]. You supply the domain name. Ask the postmaster the following questions:

   - What year was the Internet connection made?
   - How many connections are made to the Internet on a daily basis?
   - What does the connection cost annually?
   - How fast is the number of users growing?

   Or, ask the postmaster anything you want! Just get mail to and back from that person.

3. Send yourself an e-mail message and a copy to your instructor.

4. Create a nickname for yourself and two other classmates and place them on the Quick Recipient list. Now delete the nickname you created for yourself.

5. Create the following signature, attach it to the following message and send the message to a classmate.

```
Dear Classmate—Finally, I get to send e-mail!
**************************************

*:-) Let a smile be your umbrella :-)*
**************************************
```

5

Using ftp: Getting Information Off the Internet

After completing this chapter, you will be able to

- Understand what ftp is and how it is used
- Use Netscape and WS_FTP to ftp
- Connect to a host computer to find files
- Locate a file you want to download and download it
- Navigate through directories and subdirectories to find files
- Tell the difference between binary and ASCII files
- Download single or multiple files
- Use e-mail to get files

Now that you've written to the President of the United States, you're probably becoming more familiar with what the Internet has to offer and more confident with its use. If someone told you that over 10,000 recipes, the complete text of *Moby Dick*, and everything you wanted to know about the Bart Simpson family were available in one place, would you believe it? We hope the answer is yes, because all this and more is stored in files all over the Internet. But you have to know how to get to the files and the information they contain. This chapter is about using the file transfer protocol (ftp) to locate files on the Internet and transfer them to your Internet connection. From there, they can be transferred to your own personal computer.

WHAT'S FILE TRANSFER PROTOCOL, OR FTP?

File transfer protocol, or **ftp**, is both a noun and a verb. As a noun, it is the protocol or set of rules that the Internet uses to transfer a file from one location to another. As a verb, it describes the action you take when you transfer a file from one location to another. For example, you ftp to the Internet site named csd.uwm.edu to access Scott Yanoff's Special Internet Connections kit, a great starting point for anyone who wants an overview of the resources available on the Net. Sometimes, ftp sites are sometimes referred to as **anonymous ftp** sites, meaning that anyone is welcome to connect and get information. The majority of ftp sites that you will deal with are anonymous.

USING NETSCAPE AND FTP

Let's see how easy it is to ftp to a location and get the Yanoff list that is updated each month. In Chapter 3, you learned that each WWW site has a special prefix (http) before its address. The same is true for ftp sites. To get to an ftp site, enter the ftp command in the Open Location field, supply the URL, and press Enter. Let's locate and **download** the Yanoff file now. We assume that you are at the opening Netscape screen.

1. Click File and then click Open.

2. Type ftp://ftp.csd.uwm.edu and press Enter. Netscape will go to work and connect you to the opening screen for this ftp site shown in Figure 5.1. If the site is busy, usually the case during 9A.M. to 5P.M., you'll get a message telling you that the connection could not be made because the maximum number of users are connected. You'll have to try again later.

FIGURE 5.1

The ftp site csd.uwm.edu opening screen.

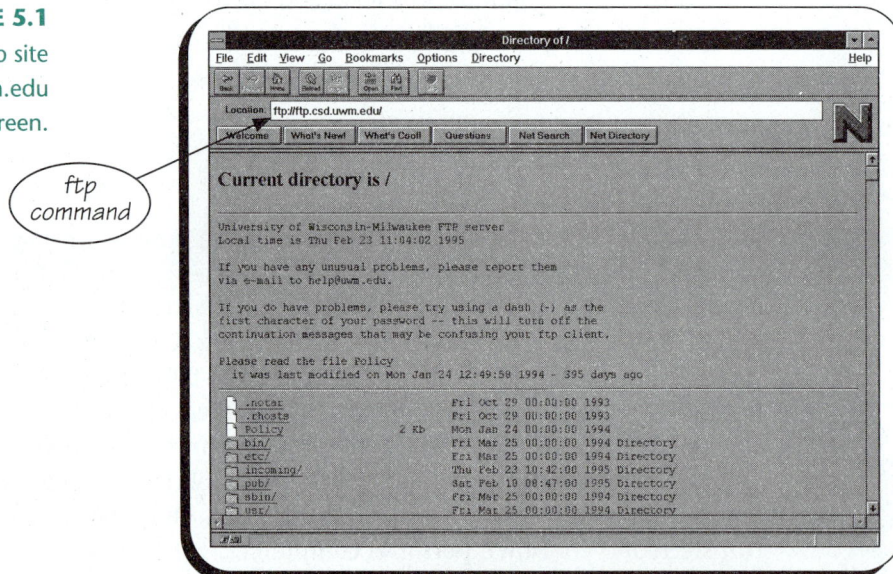

3. Click on the directory named pub. When you do this, you will see that the URL changes from csd.uwm.edu to csd.uwm.edu/pub/ since you are

now in the directory named pub. You can see what this new screen location looks like in Figure 5.2.

FIGURE 5.2

In the
ftp.csd.uwm.edu/
pub/ directory.

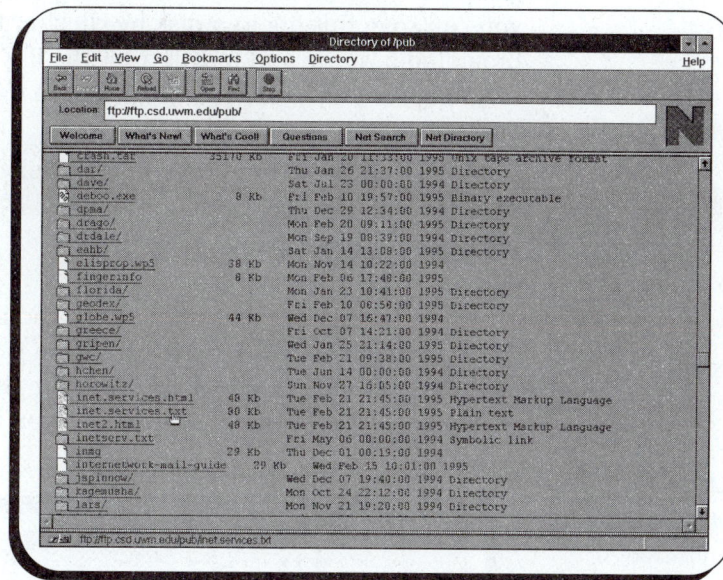

4. Click inet.services.txt. Yanoff's list of almost every subject you want to
know about appears as shown in Figure 5.3.

This is the file we are looking for. How do we know the name of the file
we want? A variety of ways: we read it in a periodical like *Internet World*,
a friend told us, someone's home page contained the ftp address and the
name of the file, and so on. If you are to be an **Internaut** or a **netizen**
(someone who uses the Internet), you have to stay on your toes with
your ears and eyes wide open.

FIGURE 5.3

The Yanoff
Special Internet
Connections list—
what a resource!

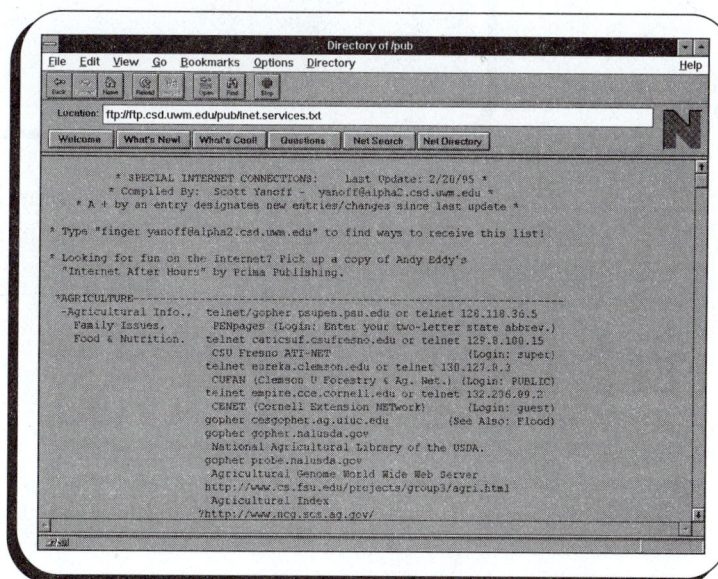

By the way, you can tell that inet.services.txt is a file since the icon for a file ⃞ looks like a page of text. The icon for a directory ⃞ looks like a folder. Now print out this file by clicking File, and then clicking Print. Or, you can save this file to a disk by clicking File, then clicking Save, and providing a name and location for the file. If you save it to a disk, you can then use your own word processor to format any changes you want and print it out.

5. Click Back on the Netscape screen. You will be returned to the screen you see in Figure 5.2.

6. Click inset.services.html.

Guess what you'll see? The html suffix should clue you in that you are looking at a home page and, as you can see in Figure 5.4, that's exactly what appears. It's Yanoff's list in HTML format, complete with a zillion links from here to there and everywhere else. Anything you're interested in, just click.

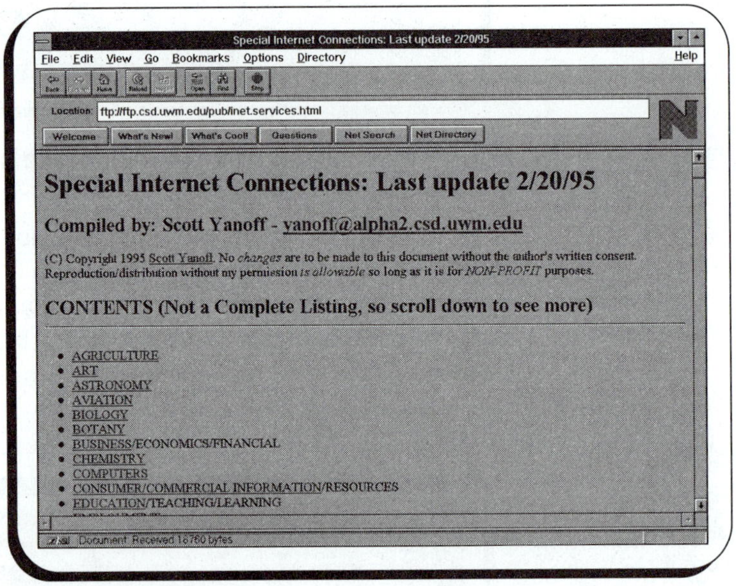

FIGURE 5.4
The Yanoff Special Internet Connection list in HTML format.

Yanoff's list is a great list to play around with and explore. As you learn more about the Internet through *Hand-Ons Internet for Windows*, you'll learn how to use these different resources.

84 Chapter 5 — Using ftp: Getting Information Off the Internet

**HOW TO FTP
IN NETSCAPE
AND GET A FILE**

1. Click File, and then click Open.

2. Type ftp followed by the full ftp site URL.

3. Press Enter.

4. Navigate through directories to find the file you want.

5. Use the Save command to transfer the file from the Internet to your computer.

**USING FTP
FOR WINDOWS**

Besides Netscape, there are other easy-to-use Windows tools for downloading files from a remote site. One is ftp for Windows. A version of ftp for Windows (WS_FTP) is available from the ftp sites listed in Appendix A. After ftp for Windows is installed, click on the icon you see here ⏣ and you will see the opening session profile screen shown in Figure 5.5.

FIGURE 5.5

ftp for Windows.

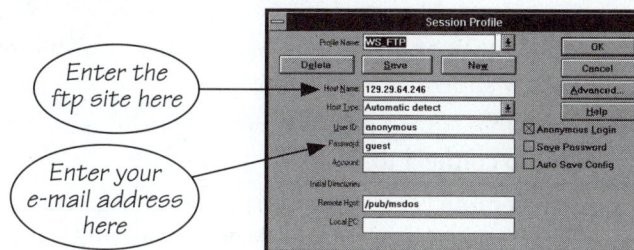

You need to provide specific information in this opening screen for ftp for Windows to work. Here's what each blank in the Session Profile screen requires. If you are in a computer lab, most of these will already be defined. If you have trouble supplying the correct information, ask your instructor. Most of the time, if WS_FTP does not work, it's because this information is incorrect.

- The **profile name** is any name you want to use to identify the connection you are creating. You can save this and return to it easily in the future.

- The **host name** is an Internet address or an IP number such as 129.29.64.246. This is where you want to connect to. In this example, we will connect to ftp.csd.uwm.edu.

- The **user ID** is your user id. As we have already mentioned, most ftp sites do not require permission and the conventional user sign-on is *anonymous*. As you don't have an actual account on the site to which you are ftping, anonymous is the standard that's used.

- The **password** is your e-mail address which allows the ftp supervisor to know who's using the system. Some ftp sites require this and some do not. If you get a *connection failed* message, click Exit and then try again, supplying your e-mail address as a password.

- The **account** is the account number you will need if the site to which you are ftping actually does require this information. In almost all cases, no such information is requested.

- The **remote host** is the path you want to connect to, which contains the file you need.

- The **local host** is the computer from which the connection is originating.

- The **local PC** is used to identify the PC you are using—you can leave this blank.

Now let's connect to the ftp site and have some fun. You should be in Windows with the WS_FTP icon 🏠 visible.

1. Double-click on the ftp for Windows icon. You'll see the Session Profile window shown in Figure 5.5.

2. Click Host Name and type ftp.csd.uwm.edu. This is the location you want to connect to.

3. Click Remote Host and type /pub, and then click OK or press Enter. After WS_FTP does its work, you'll see the opening screen shown in Figure 5.6 and you are at the ftp.csd.uwm.edu ftp site. This is your gateway to all the stuff located at this ftp site. Let's look at the elements in the screen and see what they can do.

FIGURE 5.6
The WS_FTP
opening screen.

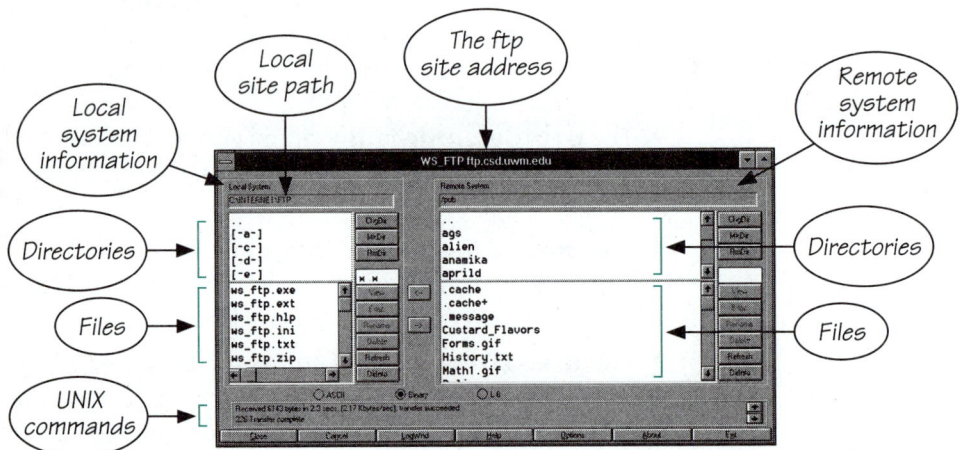

First, the screen has two mini-windows. The left side represents the **local system** or your Internet location. The right side represents the **remote system** or the ftp site to which you are connected. You can always tell what ftp site you are connected to by looking at the title bar. In this example it is WS_FTP ftp.csu.uwm.edu. The mini-windows are separated into two sections by a horizontal line. Above the line are directories which contain files. Below the line is a list of the files in the *current* directory. You can change directories by double-clicking on the name of the directory you want to change.

On the right edge of both mini-windows, you can see a bunch of buttons. Here's what they are used for. Remember, you can use any of these commands to work with files and directories on either the local or remote side of ftp.

- **ChgDir** allows you to change to a new directory. Use this command to locate the file in which you are interested in accessing.

- **MkDir** allows you to make a new directory. Use this when you want to make a new directory to store or download a file.

- **RmDir** allows you to remove a directory. Use this when you want to remove a directory.

- **View** allows you to view the contents of a file. This is a great tool to check that what you're about to transfer is what you think it is before you actually make the transfer. If you view a program file or a graphic, you'll see what looks like gobbledygook as those files are written in machine or program code. If a file is too large to view in Notebook (the Windows application that WS_FTP uses for this purpose), WS_FTP will provide a message to that effect. In this case, you will not be able to view the view until you transfer it.

- **Exec** allows you to execute a program file. If the file can be executed or run, it actually will be.

- **Rename** allows you to rename a file. Use this to rename a new file so that it is not identical or similar to an existing filename.

- **Delete** allows you to delete a file. Use this to clean up files at your local site or at a remote site—but make sure you "own" the contents at that site first.

- **Refresh** allows WS_FTP to refresh the screen. Use this when you have changed files and directory and want the screen brought up to date.

- **DirInfo** provides information about a particular directory. Use this to find out what other directories and files are present.

The commands you see at the bottom of the WS_FTP window are Unix commands (a standard technical computer language) and show what is actually happening in the background. If you want to know what these commands mean and how to use them in character-based ftp activities, see this book's companion (*Hands-On Internet*, boyd and fraser, 1995).

3. Click on the scroll bar on the Remote Side of the WS_FTP screen until you see the inet.services.txt file as shown in Figure 5.7. This is the file you are going to transfer.

FIGURE 5.7

Scrolling to locate the file you want.

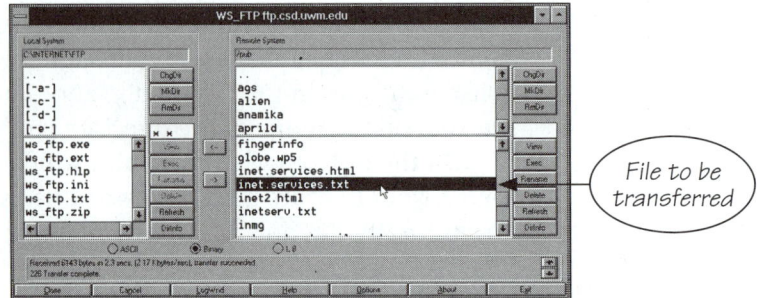

4. Click inet.services.txt. Keep in mind (once again!) that the Internet is always being reorganized and that the location of this or any other file may be different. If you cannot find a file, try other directories and explore. Usually the file is at the ftp site, but it may not be in the same folder as it was a week ago (or will be a week from today!).

5. Click ← to transfer the file. WS_FTP begins transferring the file. You'll know this by the RET (for retrieve) message that appears in the lower left-hand corner of the screen as the transfer is taking place. If you want to download more than one file, hold down the Ctrl key as you click on the individual files. Each will be highlighted and transferred when you then click ←.

As you can see in Figure 5.8, the file was transferred from the remote site (ftp.csd.uwm.edu) to the local site (c:\internet\ftp) which is a directory path on my hard drive. The reason why the file's title is inet.*ser*, rather than inet.*service.txt*, is that when the file was transferred to my hard drive, on a DOS machine, my computer truncated the extension to the three characters, *ser*.

FIGURE 5.8

Transferring a file from the remote to the local site.

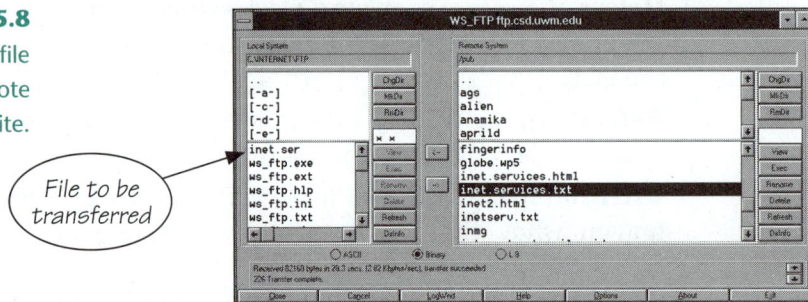

A file is transferred to whichever directory is open at the local site. By double-clicking on different directories, you can select the location where you want a file transferred. In this case, the file is transferred to c:\internet\ftp. I could have created a directory named "stuff" or "Yanoff" or whatever I wanted. Remember, this is the same file you see in Figure 5.3.

**HOW TO USE
WS_FTP TO
DOWNLOAD
A FILE**

1. Double-click on the WS_FTP icon.

2. In the Sessions Profile window, enter the Host Name.

3. In the Sessions Profile window, enter the Remote Host path to the directory which contains the file you want to download.

4. Click OK.

5. Find the file you want to download in the Remote Host side of the WS_FTP Window.

6. Click ←.

**HOW TO
DOWNLOAD
MULTIPLE FILES**

1. Open WS_FTP.

2. Locate the files you want to transfer.

3. Highlight the file you want to transfer. To select more than one file, use the Ctrl+Click move.

4. Determine the location where you want the files transferred to.

5. Type ←.

Working with Directories and Files

Once you connect to an ftp site (which is no more than using the ftp command and the site), you need to work with the directories and files at the site to locate the file (or files) you are looking for. In the above example where we looked for the file named inet.services.txt, we went directly to the correct directory. When we used Netscape, we had to go to the directory named *pub* which contained the file we wanted.

Often, however, the file you want is located within a directory that is part of another directory and so forth. For example, as you can see in Figure 5.9, the file inet.services.txt is located in the directory named *pub* which was accessed at the ftp site named owl.nstn.ns.ca (another Internet location containing the Yanoff list). On the other hand, if you want a current white pages of e-mail addresses of people on the Internet, you would ftp to the site named MsState.edu and go through a set of directories including the directory named *pub*, then the directory named *docs*, and then get the file named *finding-addresses*.

FIGURE 5.9

Finding files
includes looking in
one or more than
one directory.

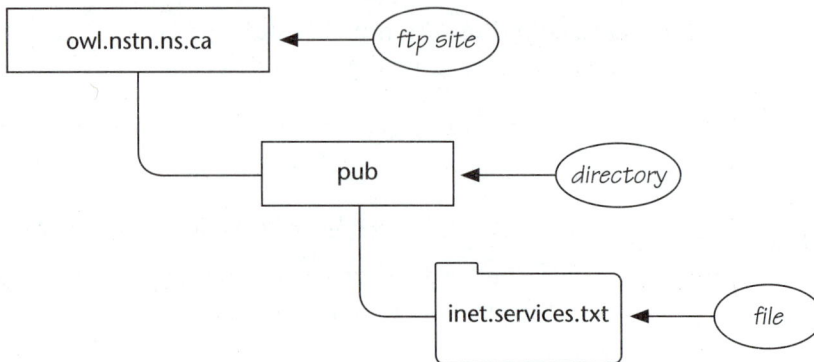

The fact that files are located in various levels of ftp sites means that in order to use ftp effectively, you need the skills to navigate through directories. We next turn our attention to these skills.

Hierarchy of Directories and Files

Files on the Internet are organized in directories and subdirectories. A **directory** is a collection of subdirectories and may also contain files. A **subdirectory** can be a collection of other subdirectories and files as well. Technically, there is only one main directory and that's at the topmost level of the file organization chart. Everything below that is a subdirectory.

As you can see in Figure 5.10, the one main directory is also called the **root directory** located the top of the hierarchy. Within this directory are other directories (subdirectory 1, subdirectory 2, subdirectory 3, and subdirectory 4), and within each of these directories are files. And as we just explained, some subdirectories (such as subdirectory #4) can contain other subdirectories (such as subdirectory #5).

FIGURE 5.10

How directories and
files are organized
on the internet.

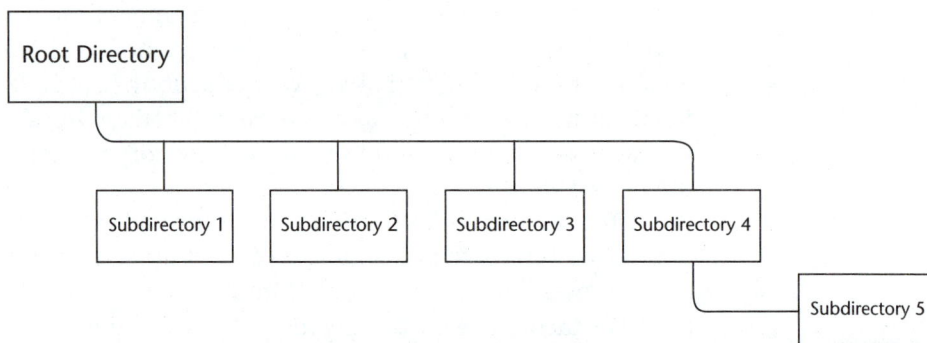

In Figure 5.11 you can see a graphic of our search for another must-have Internet file named **bigfun.txt**. This is Big Fun on the Internet with Uncle Bert, full of places to go and things to do—from the results of the latest Harris Poll to the periodic table to the text of the lyrics of popular songs. The file bigfun.txt is within the subdirectory named netinfo which, in turn, is in the directory named pub.

FIGURE 5.11
Directories often contain other directories.

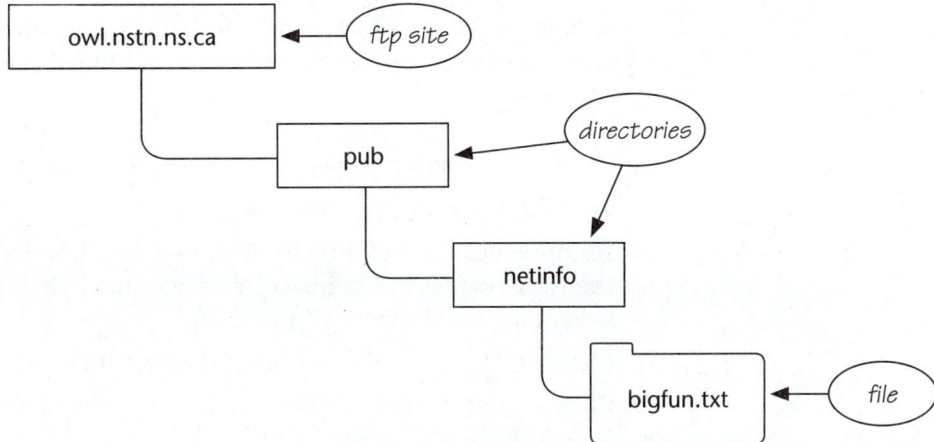

When you first ftp to a site, you are at the root or highest level of organization unless you enter a path to some other directory in the Remote Host field in the Sessions Profile dialog box as shown in Figure 5.6. Let's explore the structure of files and directories as we download the file named bigfun.txt.

Navigating Through Files And Directories

We're going to ftp to the site that contains bigfun.txt and click on the buttons that will take us to the file we want.

1. In the Sessions Profile dialog box you saw in Figure 5.5, type owl.nstn.ns.ca in the Host Name field and click OK.

FIGURE 5.12
Connecting to owl.nstn.ns.ca.

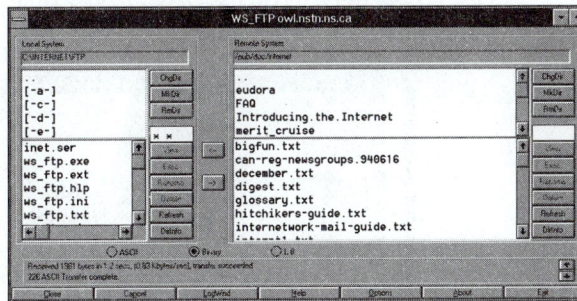

2. Click in the Remote Host field.
3. Type /pub/doc/Internet, and then press Enter.

Once you connect, the opening screen should appear as shown in Figure 5.12. You should see bigfun.txt in the files section of the remote screen. If you don't, scroll through the screen. By typing the complete path, you are avoiding having to click through the various directories to get to the directory (Internet) where the file named bigfun.txt is located. The **path** is the series of steps in the hierarchy to a particular location. Rather than clicking pub and then clicking doc and then clicking netinfo, to reach the location where the file bigfun.txt was located, you used the path command and typed pub/doc/internet at the remote command.

4. On the local system side of WS_FTP, click MkDir.

5. Type bigfun, and then click OK.

6. Double-click on the directory named BIGFUN you just created. Since there are no files in this new directory named BIGFUN, you'll see a blank lower portion of the local host screen.

7. Click bigfun.txt on the remote side of WS_FTP.

8. Click ← and the file will be transferred to the directory named BIGFUN as you see in Figure 5.13.

FIGURE 5.13

Transferring bigfun.txt from a remote location to the BIGFUN directory at the local host.

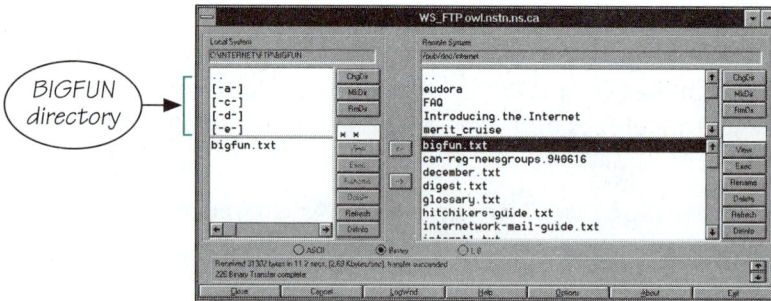

You can also get to and see bigfun by entering the following line in the Netscape URL (see Figure 5.14):

```
ftp://owl.nstn.ns.ca/pub/doc/Internet/bigfun.txt
```

FIGURE 5.14

The bigfun.txt file.

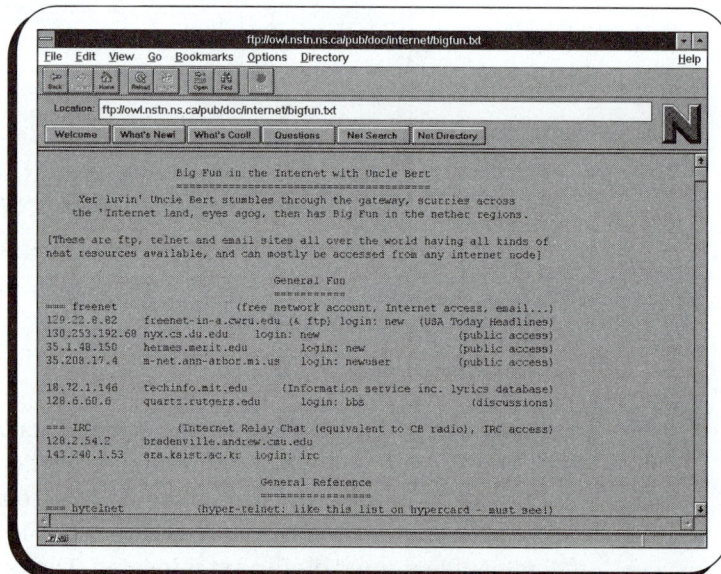

You can then print or save it as we discussed earlier. Using ftp in Netscape is just another way to get to the same place. This method demonstrates how you can quickly see the contents of a file from an ftp site and then print or save it once it's downloaded.

WHICH TYPE OF FILE DO I HAVE?

In the WS_FTP window, there are three buttons—ASCII, Binary, and L8—all used to signify different types of files you will find at any ftp site. The ← button transfers a file from the ftp site to your Internet connection where you can get to a rich diversity of files located on the Internet on just about anything you can imagine. But, these files are also stored in different formats. Basically, there are two types of Internet files and each one needs to be treated in a different fashion in order for the download to be successful.

Identifying ASCII or Text Files

The first type of format is called **ASCII**. These files use the American Standard Code for Information Interchange. Almost any other application (such as Word-Perfect or Excel) can read an ASCII file. It makes sense to work with ASCII files whenever possible since they are easily used once transferred. If you see a file with a *.txt* extension at the end of the filename, you can be sure it's stored as an ASCII file. The same is true for files named *read.me*. WS_FTP is set at a default to transfer files in ASCII format. Unless you tell it otherwise, it will assume the file is in that format. Netscape knows what the file is and brings it to your screen accordingly. From there, you can download it to your computer or print it.

Identifying Binary Files

The second type of file is called a **binary file**. These are files that have been created using a particular application such as WordPerfect or Excel and can only be read using these programs. These are sometimes called program files. Sound, graphic files, and programs are almost always stored in binary format.

Telling the Difference Between File Types

How can you tell whether a file is ASCII or binary? Here are some guidelines.

1. In general, filenames without an extension—such as spaghetticarbonara (if the operating system used allows more than eight characters in a filename)—are usually in ASCII format. But, remember that ASCII filenames sometimes have extensions like bigfun.txt.
2. When a file has a .txt extension, it is definitely in ASCII format.
3. Programs and documents created with applications such as word processors, databases, spreadsheets, and graphics are almost always binary.

Not sure about the file type? Transfer it as a binary file. ASCII files, transferred as binary files, transfer just fine. It's only when you try to transfer a binary file as an ASCII file that you'll get unintelligible gibberish on your screen. Before you download or transfer a file, you have to click on either ASCII or Binary to tell WS_FTP what kind of file you are working with. L8 is a special type of format which should not concern you at this point.

About Compressed Files

Many files on the Internet are **compressed** to save space. This means that you have to decompress them in order to use them. Many compression utilities (such as pkzip.exe) create their own unique extensions when they are used to compress a file and you're likely to see lots of these around the Net. Table 5.1 lists some extensions, the file type, and name of the utility used to decompress the file. It's beyond the scope of this book to go into great detail about any one type of compression, but you will need a program to decompress files in order to use a binary file. Where can you find these programs? On the Internet, where else? We'll talk about finding files in Chapter 8.

TABLE 5.1   Extensions and decompression utilities

Extension	File Type	Utility used to compress the file
arc	binary	arc
doc	ASCII	none needed
lzh	binary	lharc
zip	binary	PKZIP
txt	ASCII	none needed
readme	ASCII	none needed
gif	binary	none needed but you need a graphical interchange format file reader
exe	binary	self-extracting file created by various utilities such as lharc and PKZIP
sit	binary	StuffIt

NO FTP? MAIL AWAY!   Not all systems have ftp. If yours does not, all is not lost—you can use e-mail tools to download a file. However, you won't have the convenience of being able to search through various directories to find files you might want to download. Rather than browsing through the kitchen of goodies, you have to place an order with someone else. You have to know the location of the file, that is, the complete file path and name of the file you want.

To get files through e-mail, you have to use an **ftpmail server**. You send them a message, and they send you back the files via e-mail. Here are the steps you need to follow if you were to e-mail (which is what you do) to an ftpmail server and order the file named inet.services.txt which we downloaded earlier in this chapter. It's an alternative way to downloading files. To use an ftpmail server you have to send mail, so close WS_FTP if you are still in it (click Exit) and open Eudora.

1. Type ftpmail@pa.dec.com in the To: field.
2. In the Message Text area of Eudora, type the following lines:
   connect csd4.csd.uwm.edu
   cd pub
   get inet.services.txt
   quit

   The connect command tells the ftpmail server to connect to the ftp site that contains the files you want. The get command identifies the site containing the files we need. ftpmail@pa.dec.com is one of several ftp mail servers. Others can be found at mail-server@rtfm.mit.edu and bitftp@PUCC.Princeton.edu. You'll get back a message from the ftpmail server giving you information about the size of the transmissions and how far back in the line you are. The file you requested, inet.services.txt, will eventually arrive by mail. If you have ftp, use it. But if you don't, it does not mean you are stuck not being able to download files you need.

TEN INTERESTING FTP SITES

Look at the diversity of topics covered in these ten sites where you can find fun and valuable information. Want more? Just glance at Yanoff's list and bigfun. Be sure to put aside lots of time to explore as ftping is very addictive. Keep in mind, however, that these are very busy sites and you may not be able to get connected. Try again later. Also keep in mind that the Internet is *always* changing, and what is available at one moment may not be available in ten minutes.

1. Want some great pictures? ftp to wuarchive.wustl.edu
2. Want to see the earth from the space shuttle? ftp to sseop.jsc.nasa.gov
3. Want enough recipes to last you the rest of 1994 (if not your life)? ftp to gatekeeper.dec.com
4. Want to visit the pop music electronic mecca? ftp to mtv.com
5. Want to learn about juggling? ftp to piggy.cogsci.indiana.edu
6. Want to read *Peter Pan*? ftp to mrcnext.cso.uiuc.edu
7. Awesome, dude. All about Bart Simpson and his family. ftp to ftp.cs.widener.edu
8. Want a giant list of listserv groups? ftp to lilac.berkeley.edu
9. Want to have access to tons of software? ftp to oak.oakland.edu
10. Want to get started brewing your own beer? ftp to mthvax.cs.miami.edu

There are tens of thousands upon thousands of ftp sites where you can get files to download. If you really want to have fun, look at Scott Yanoff's list. And, don't forget to keep your eyes and ears open. Talk to the people on the Net. They're sure to know about some wild (and useful!) ftp sites.

FTP NETIQUETTE   While ftping is great fun, if has its share of rules and regulations, just as e-mail and any other element of the Internet. See Box 5.1 for our guidelines for behaviour when using ftp.

BOX 5.1

Guidelines for
ftp Netiquette.

1. When asked for your account number, use the word *anonymous*.

2. When asked for your password, use your full e-mail account. This allows the ftp site managers to track who's using what files. It's also just polite. You know who they are so they should know who you are.

3. If you have to download a giant file, do it during off hours like early morning or late at night. Otherwise you tie up resources that people might need for only a few minutes.

4. Once a file is transferred to the host system to which you are connected, download it to your own system so that you free up resources on the host.

5. When the ftp site supervisor tells you not to spend more than 15 minutes on-line, adhere to his or her wishes. If there are such time restrictions, then it must be a very busy site. If you (and others) don't adhere, the site will eventually become a non-anonymous one where you can't just check in.

6. You may be downloading files that are copyrighted, shareware, or some other author arrangement. Make sure you read the read.me file or the documentation that accompanies the text or executable files. Be sure you don't violate anybody else's expressed wishes.

Dear Miss Manners:

I am becoming increasingly frustrated with the fact that there are zillions of files at the ftp sites I go to. Please, how is it possible for one to know what's there?

Stranded on the Net

Dear Gentle Reader:

I can well sympathize with your dilemma. I, too, have found myself watching hundreds of files whiz by on my screen without any knowledge of what each one contains. I suggest you download the file named readme or read.me. These files often contain detailed information about what's contained in the directories which they accompany.

miss.manners@benice.com

The Internet is a gold mine of information, and the tool you need to find that gold is ftp. With it, you can go around the corner or around the world to get information about almost anything or find computer programs that will do exactly what you need. Now that you're introduced to ftp and what it can do, let's look for other sources of information in the newsgroups that are as important a part of the Internet as ftp. That's what we'll do in the next chapter.

KEY WORDS

account
anonymous ftp
ASCII
bigfun.txt
binary file
Ch3Dir
Delete
directory
DirInfo
download
Exec
file transfer protocol or ftp
ftp
ftpmail server
host name
Internaut
local system

local PC
local host
MkDir
netizen
password
path
profile name
Rename
Refresh
remote host
remote system
RmDir
root directory
subdirectory
user ID
View

REVIEW QUESTIONS

1. There are at least two ways to get a file from another location. What are the two, what is the difference between them, and why use one versus the other?

2. When you ftp to a site using WS_FTP, you may be required to provide an address. What is this address and why would you be asked to provide such information?

3. What do the following WS_FTP buttons do and when are they used?

   Ch3Dir

   MkDir

   ←

4. If the path to a file is doctor/medical/time.txt, what is the highest level of this path? What format is the file time.txt? How do you know?

5. If you wanted to download all the files from a particular ftp site, how would you do it?

6. What is a compressed file and how do you know that a file you get from an ftp site is compressed?

EXPLORATION EXERCISES

1. Download the Big Dummy Guide (named bigfun.txt). Who wrote the foreword?

2. Use the Yanoff list to ftp to ftp.uwp.edu and find out what the fourth line of lyrics is for the song "Swing Low, Sweet Chariot."

3. Use the Yanoff list to ftp to ds.internic.net and look in the path pub/the-scientist. How many questions are in the questionnaire? Who is the editor?

Newsgroups:
All the News, All the Time

After completing this chapter, you'll be able to

- Identify different newsgroups and what they contain
- Start and use Netscape and NewsXpress to read news from newsgroups
- Subscribe and unsubscribe to newsgroups
- Manage, save, and mail articles
- Insert an article in a newsgroup
- Insert a follow-up to an article
- Sign on to a mailing list

There are two kinds of computer users: those who have lost data and those who will. The other day, while working on *Hands-On Internet for Windows* I accidentally deleted an important file. As I was about to reconcile myself to starting over, I remembered a newsgroup named comp.arch.storage (all about computers and storage). Using Netscape or NewsXpress, my handy news readers, I went to that group, found an article about undeleting files, and e-mailed the author with a specific question about my problem. Within a few hours, I had an answer to the question and the solution to my problem.

E-mail is great for keeping in touch with friends and ftp provides you with the capability to go around the world and get files that contain programs, information, graphics, and sounds. Now we'll concentrate on what might be the most interactive part of the Internet—newsgroups. A newsgroup is like a meeting about a particular topic on the Internet. Whether it be juggling, adoption, baked Alaska, the Allman Brothers, or recovering data—there's a group talking about it on the Internet. In this chapter, we'll show you how to work with newsgroups including contributing your own news.

WHAT IS NEWS?

Imagine being able to find information about 30,000 topics ranging from stereo systems to jokes (censored and otherwise) to the ethics of law to college football to astronomy. Where in the world would you be able to find a collection of such diverse information that can be easily accessed? You guessed it—the Internet and the various **USENET** sites that ship news around the world each day. The news that fits in one category, such as college football or the ethics of law, forms a newsgroup (also called a group). A **newsgroup** is simply a collection of information about the same topic.

USENET started in North Carolina in 1980 when two students wrote a program to automatically transfer information on a topic from one computer to another. In other words, once information was posted in the form of a file on one computer, it would automatically be sent to another, then another, then another. And along the way, new news articles would be picked up and sent along as you see happening in Figure 6.1.

FIGURE 6.1
How news is distributed and read.

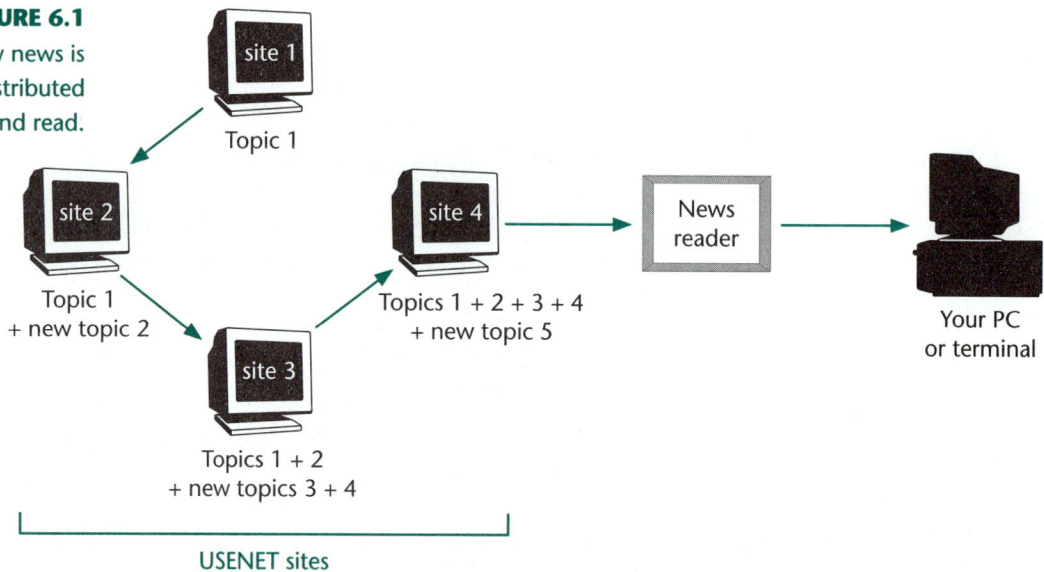

site 1
Topic 1

site 2
Topic 1
+ new topic 2

site 3
Topics 1 + 2
+ new topics 3 + 4

site 4
Topics 1 + 2 + 3 + 4
+ new topic 5

News reader

Your PC or terminal

USENET sites

In Figure 6.1, topic 1 starts at site 1 and is sent to site 2. There, topic 2 is picked up and both topics 1 and 2 are sent off to site 3. There, topics 3 and 4 are picked up and, together, they are sent along with topics 1 and 2 to site 4. This continues until all the sites on the USENET tour have picked up and delivered news. Then, using the Internet **news reader** tool (what you use to read news), you can read the news on your PC or terminal.

Now, in 1995, there are more than 30,000 sites or connections on the huge USENET network. This means there are 30,000 places that send out news each day and the same 30,000 pick up news from other locations. To help manage the flow of articles, news sites are managed, moderated, administered, and censored by system administrators. However, not all newsgroups reach each potential site or everyone who has access to an Internet site. The newsgroups from which you can select news are those that the system administrator makes available.

Before you begin learning about news in this chapter, there's one thing you need to know about how it is structured. Newsgroups and the news they contain change even from minute to minute. So far in *Hands-On Internet for Windows*, many of the screen examples you have seen may have matched what appears on your monitor screen. That's even less likely to happen here—for two reasons. First, because you may not have access to the same newsgroups that I do. And second, even if you do, the structure of those newsgroups is probably different from what was available when this book was written. Don't let the fact that there is a difference unduly concern you. Just continue to read and practice using newsgroups with what you have available.

What's in the News?

When we talked about e-mail (Chapter 4), you saw how e-mail addresses can have domain names such as *.edu* or *.org* in common. The same is true for newsgroups. Although there are not many restrictions as to what goes on within a newsgroup except for the system administrator's management, the way newsgroups are named and organized follows a set of rules.

The Major Newsgroups

The most general of these rules has to do with the name of the group itself. Like domain names, there is a hierarchical structure to a newsgroup name, with the highest level of the hierarchy appearing in the left-most position. For example, as you can see in Figure 6.2, the newsgroup name rec.sport.football.college means that within *rec* (the general name for the recreation newsgroup), there is a subset named *sport*, and within that another subset named *football* and within that another subset named *college*.

FIGURE 6.2

How a newsgroup name is organized.

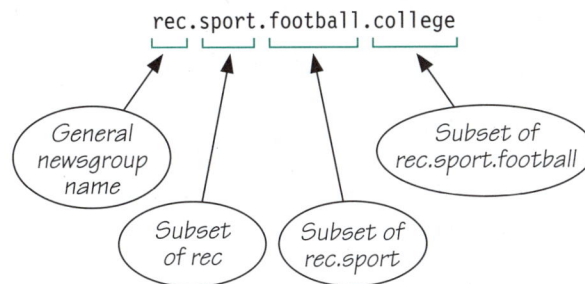

There are seven major newsgroups, each using a specific label for the first level of the hierarchy. Table 6.1 shows what these groups are named and examples of what's in each of these categories.

TABLE 6.1   The names of the main newsgroups, their general area of focus, and examples.

Newsgroup Name	General Area of Focus	Example Newsgroups
comp	Information about computers, computer science, software, and general interest computer topics.	• comp.ai (artificial intelligence) • comp.lang.c (the C programming language) • comp.bbs.misc (bulletin boards)
news	Information about news, newsgroups, and the newsgroup network	• news.adm (administering news) • news.ao.members (members of a particular newsgroup)
rec	Information about recreation, hobbies, the performing arts, hobbies, and fun stuff	• rec.sports.football (for those football nuts among us) • rec.arts.movies (movie reviews and discussion) • rec.audio (high-fidelity audio)
sci	Information about science, scientific research and discoveries, engineering, and some social science stuff	• sci.astro (astronomy) • sci.med (medicine) • sci.skeptic (UFOs and other neat speculations)
soc	Information about the social sciences	• soc.history (history) • soc.roots (genealogy) • soc.women (topics related to women)
talk	Forums on controversial topics and issues of debate	• talk.abortion (abortion) • talk.rumors (rumor control) • talk.religion (religious topics)
misc	Everything else that does not easily fit into one of the above categories	• misc.taxes (taxes) • misc.jobs (employment) • misc.fitness (physical fitness)

The Alternative Newsgroups

What you see in Table 6.1 is a listing of all the major newsgroups. There is also an alternative set of newsgroups, some of which are even more popular than main newsgroups. These alternative groups, shown in Table 6.2, are very active and can provide you with valuable information.

TABLE 6.2 The names of the alternative newsgroups, their general area of focus, and examples.

Alternative Newsgroup	General Area of Focus
alt	anything somewhat out of the ordinary
bionet	biology
bit	the BITNET e-mail network
biz	business
clari	newsgroup specific category not covered by any others
de	information in German
fj	information in Japanese
gnu	a project run by the Free Software Foundation
ieee	electrical engineering
k-12	kindergarten through 12 subjects of interest
relcom	Russian language
umsnet	the VMS computer system

Now you know what to expect based on the label used at the beginning of a newsgroup name.

An Overview of How News Works

Now down to the business of using newsgroups. A newsgroup is organized as you see in Figure 6.3. Most news readers allow you to work with news in these three groups as well, although not all. And, while most newsgroups are organized like this, not all of them are.

FIGURE 6.3
How a newsgroup and its contents are organized.

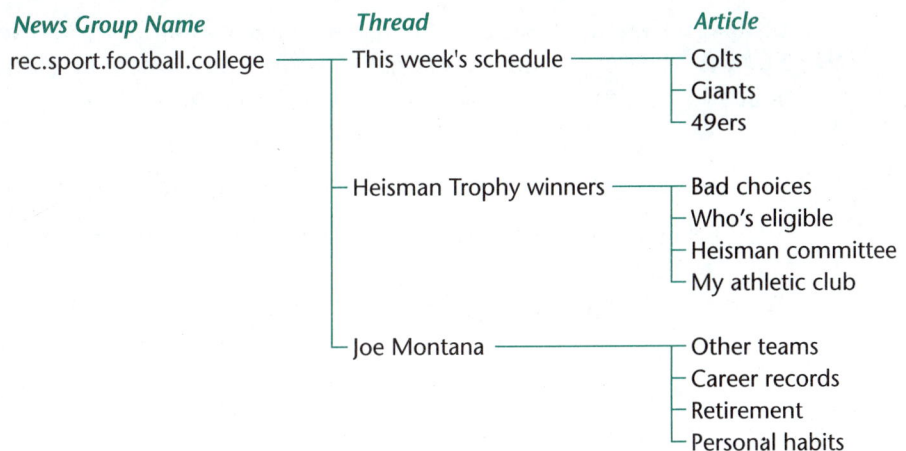

News Group Name	Thread	Article
rec.sport.football.college	This week's schedule	Colts
		Giants
		49ers
	Heisman Trophy winners	Bad choices
		Who's eligible
		Heisman committee
		My athletic club
	Joe Montana	Other teams
		Career records
		Retirement
		Personal habits

At the topmost level is the entire newsgroup itself, such as the one you see in Figure 6.3 named `rec.sport.football.college` that focuses on college football. At the next level down, you will find threads. A **thread**, such as `This week's schedule` or `Heisman Trophy Winners` is a collection of articles related to the same general topic—college football (in this case, the focus of the newsgroup named rec.sport.football.college). At the next level down you will find an article, such as "This week's schedule will be seen on. . . ." An **article** is a contribution made by an individual such as you or I. The article level is the level at which Internet users can participate in newsgroups by contributing their own articles containing new ideas, random thoughts, and general information. You'll also find that different news readers provide you with different amounts of information. Some just have groups and, within each group, a listing of articles.

What distinguishes these three important newsgroup elements from one another? Basically, their scope or breadth. For example, as you can see in Figure 6.3, a newsgroup such as rec.sport.football.college is very broad and contains different threads within that newsgroup, each of which is a bit narrower in focus than the topic of the newsgroup itself. Threads within a newsgroup are not as broad as the newsgroup they belong to. Articles are even more specific in their focus. Indeed, as a competent news user, you will begin with a newsgroup and work your way down to threads and articles. As you will see later in this chapter, it is at the thread and article level that you can perform such operations as print, save, and mail threads and articles and also contribute your own. To see how a newsgroup works, let's follow an example of someone interested in finding out about the television show "Mystery Science Theater 3000." We'll be using the feature of Netscape that reads news and deals only with newsgroups and articles.

USING NETSCAPE NEWS

Netscape and news is as simple a combination as Netscape and mail and Netscape and browsing. Once you know where and what to click, you can be reading news about your favorite topic in no time.

Starting the Netscape News Feature

To start using newsgroups in Netscape, follow this instruction:

Click Directory, and then click Go To Newsgroups as you see in Figure 6.4. This the first step you take to get to the Netscape news feature.

FIGURE 6.4
Starting
Netscape
news.

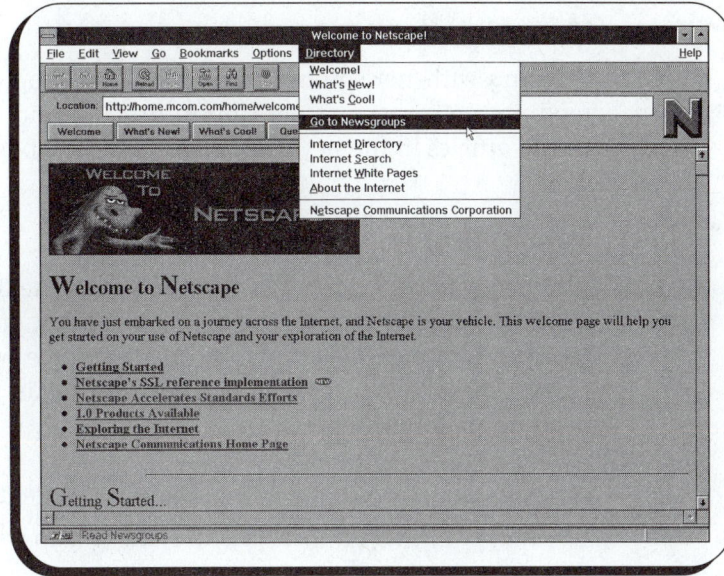

Once the connection has been made to your Internet news site, you'll see the window shown in Figure 6.5. This is a listing of the newsgroups to which you may be already **subscribed**. When you are subscribed to a newsgroup, it means that you automatically receive news about that group and Netscape keeps a record listing of which newsgroups you subscribe to. When you are **unsubscribed** to a newsgroup, it means that you do not receive news from that newsgroup. At most Internet sites, however, there are some basic newsgroups that everyone is automatically subscribed to, for example, news.announce.newuser. These usually have to do with system business and are especially helpful for novices and **newbies** (new Internet users).

FIGURE 6.5
The Netscape
screen with a
listing of
subscribed
newsgroups.

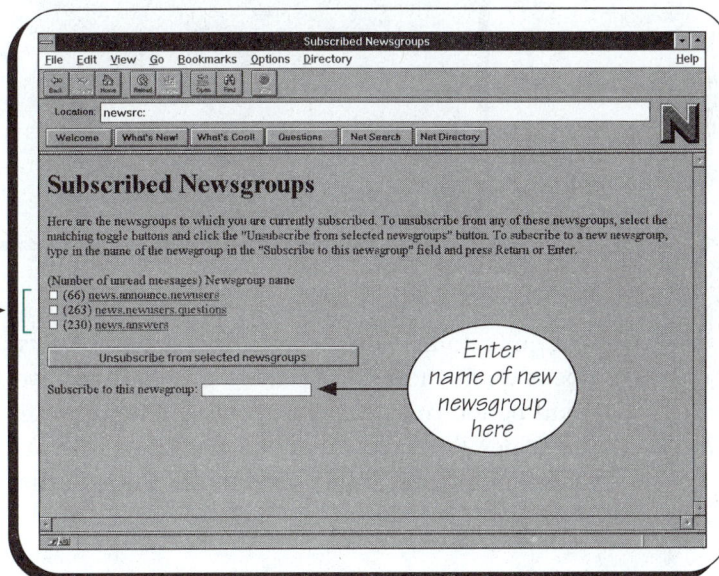

Managing Newsgroups

Working with newsgroups involves subscribing and unsubscribing to them, reading the content of newsgroup articles, and interacting with people who create articles in the newsgroup. We'll turn to all these skills now.

Subscribing to a Newsgroup

When you subscribe to a newsgroup, you are telling the news reader that you want the option to see all the news about that group. You can subscribe to as many newsgroups as you want and Netscape will list them all on the Subscribed Newsgroups opening window you see in Figure 6.5. To subscribe to a newsgroup, follow these steps.

1. Click the Subscribe to this newsgroup: field.
2. Type alt.tv.mst3k. This is the newsgroup we are using as an example.
3. Press Enter. Once you press enter, Netscape begins to work and will list the newsgroup as part of your subscribed list as you see in Figure 6.6.

FIGURE 6.6

Adding a newsgroup to the Subscribed newsgroup list.

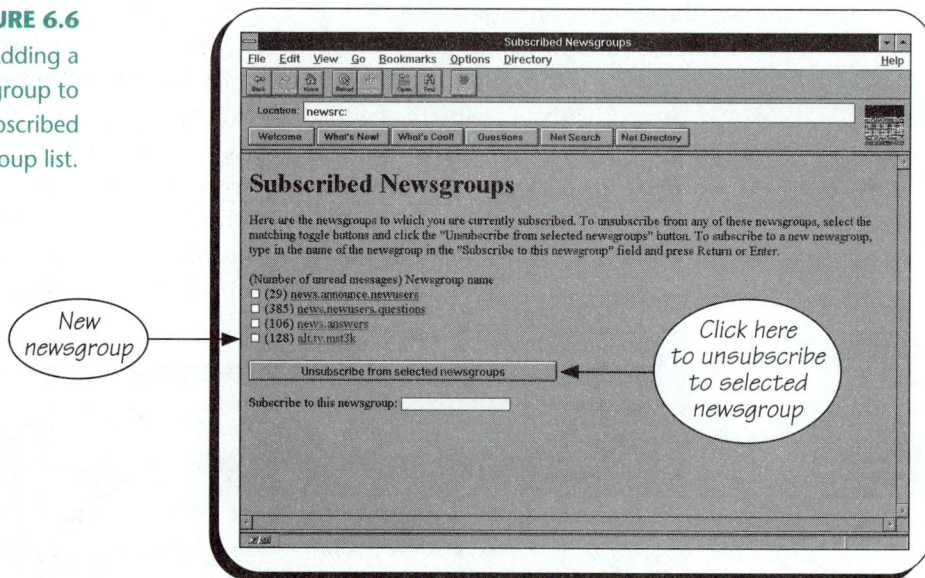

Where did we get the name alt.tv.mst3k? Since Netscape does not list all the newsgroups that are available (as does NewsXpress, the news reader we will focus on in the second part of this chapter), we kept our ears and eyes open, read periodicals, talked with other Internet users, and came up with a whole list of news sites we would like to visit. As with many other facets of the Internet, much of the best stuff is informally shared among users.

Unsubscribing to a Newsgroup

You may find that you want to unsubscribe to a newsgroup, and that's just as easy as subscribing. Unsubscribing may occur when a newsgroup is no longer of interest to you, or the newsgroup may even go defunct—no one will be creating any news! To unsubscribe to a newsgroup, follow these steps:

1. Click in [the box to the left of the newsgroup] to select it.
2. Click the Unsubscribe from selected newsgroups button. The newsgroup you selected will be unsubscribed to and, although the news will come to your Internet site, it will never come to you. If you want to unsubscribe to more than one newsgroup, then click in more than one box.

Opening a Newsgroup

Your first step in working with news is being able to see the various articles that are available in any newsgroup. To do that, you have to open the newsgroup. Place the mouse pointer on the newsgroup title (the mouse pointer will turn into a hand) and click once. As you can see in Figure 6.7, you will find yourself in the selected newsgroup window with the listing of the current articles (for example, "MSTed:various shorts (2/3)", etc.) and the contributing authors of the article. You see the listing for articles 46543 through 46577. If you want to see earlier articles, click on (Earlier articles...).

FIGURE 6.7

The newsgroup and a partial listing of articles in that newsgroup.

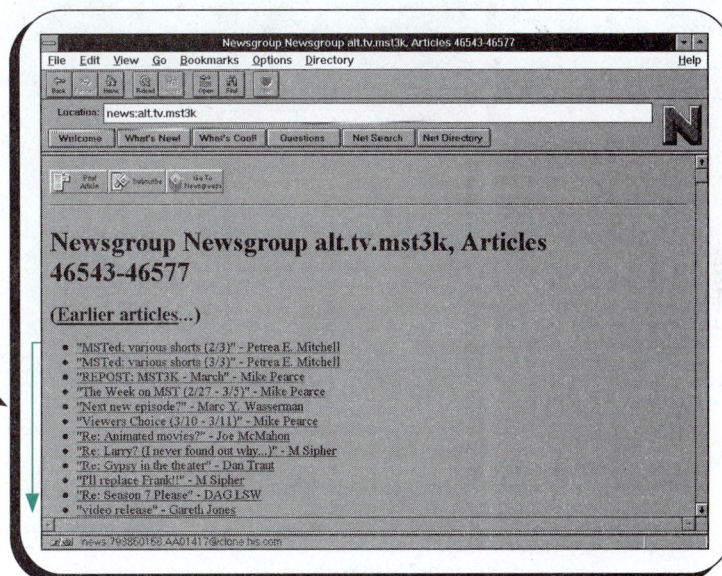

Articles in alt.tv.mst3k newsgroup

In this newsgroup you see a list of articles, but you'll also see three buttons at the top of the newsgroup screen.

- Post Article allows you to **post** an article to that newsgroup. This is the most important button of the three.
- Subscribe allows you to subscribe to that newsgroup by returning you to the Subscribed Newsgroups window.
- Go to Newsgroup returns you to the newsgroup screen you see in Figure 6.6.

The Post Article Button: Posting an Article in a Newsgroup

You don't have to necessarily read newsgroup articles to post an article yourself. You might find that you want to make a contribution before you even read one article in a group. To post an article in a newsgroup, follow these steps.

1. Click Post Article. When you do this, you will see the USENET News Posting window as shown in Figure 6.8.

FIGURE 6.8

Posting an article in a newsgroup.

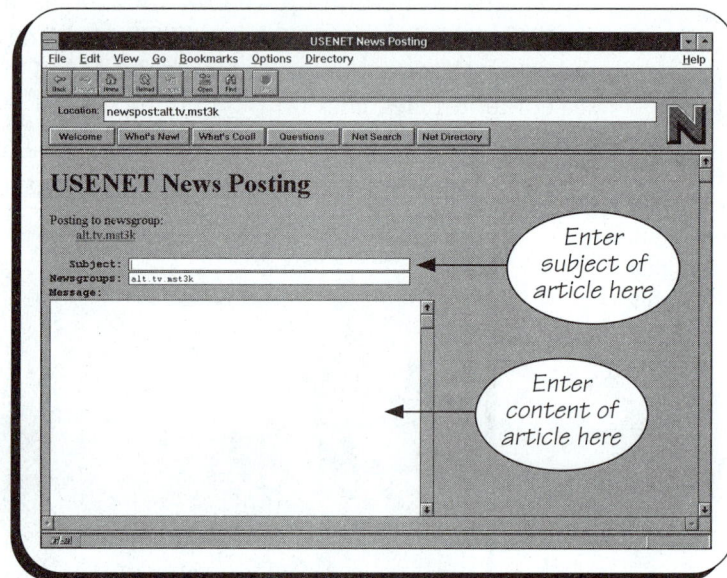

2. Click the Subject: field and enter a subject. Since you are posting an article to a specific newsgroup, the Newsgroups: field is already filled in.
3. Click the Message: field and enter [a message].
4. Click alt.tv.mst3k and the article will be posted to the newsgroup. You will not see your article posted, until you connect with Netscape news the next time. Your article will become part of the Netscape.

Reading an Article

Now it's time to examine the contents of an article contained in the newsgroup and learn how to read and work with it. Working with articles is the meat and potatoes of using news. It allows you to get into the flow of what's happening and make your own contributions. Here is where you can become an active part of the Net. To read the contents of a particular article, here's what to do:

Click on [the article title]. In this example, we clicked on "The Week on MST (2/27–3/5)" shown in Figure 6.7. What we saw was the screen shown in Figure 6.9 which displays the contents of the article.

FIGURE 6.9

The contents of one article in the newsgroup alt.tv.mst3k.

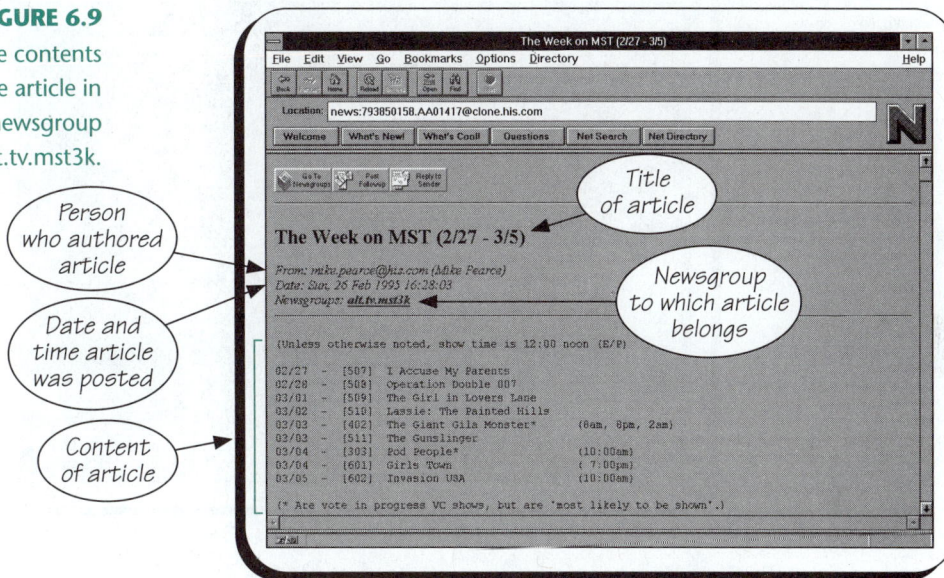

You can find important information other than information in the article itself. At the top of the article the From: field indicates who authored the article, the Date: field tells you when it was posted, and the Newsgroup: field tells you the newsgroup which this article is part of. Like other Netscape entries, the newsgroup name is underlined. If you click on it, you will be returned to the newsgroup listing of all the articles in that group. You can also see a set of buttons at the top of the article window.

- Go To Newsgroups will take you to the Subscribed Newsgroup window.

- Post Followup allows you to post a **follow-up** to an article. Remember you just posted an article; this is a follow-up to a specific article.

- Reply to Sender allows you to send mail to the person who originally authored the article (Mike Pearce in this example). Keep in mind that when you post a follow-up, everyone who looks at the article can see what you've contributed. When you reply by mail, only the author of the article sees your message.

Posting a Follow-Up

If you want to follow up on the contents of an article and add to what was said, carry out these steps.

1. Click Post Followup. In this example, we clicked on "The Week on MST (2/27–3/5)". When you do this, you will see the USENET News Posting window as shown in Figure 6.10. In the window is the content of the article.

FIGURE 6.10

Posting a follow-up to an article.

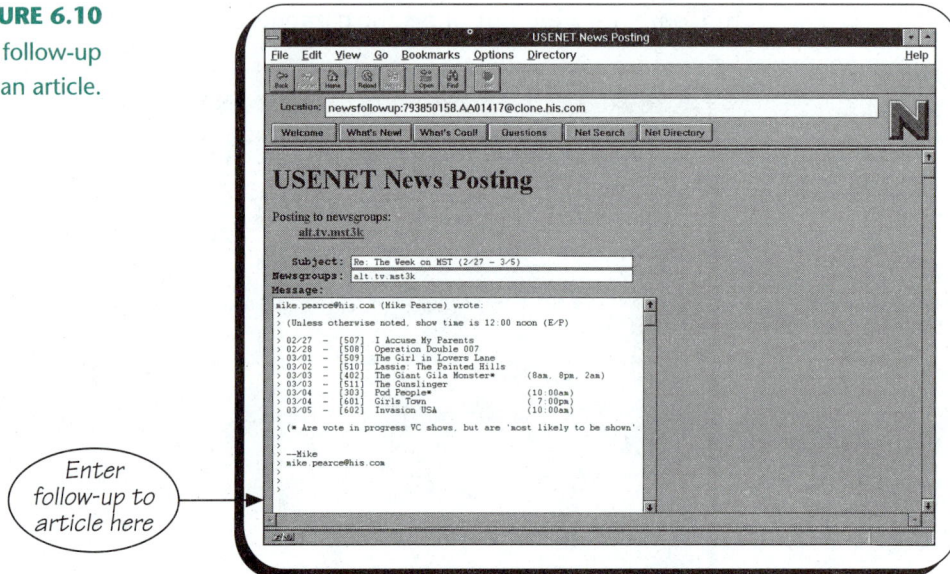

Enter follow-up to article here

2. Click at [the end of the article contents].
3. Type the follow-up you want to add to the article.
4. Scroll to the bottom of the screen and click Post Message. The follow-up will be added to the message for anyone who reads this article to see.

Replying to an Article

You may come across an interesting article and would like to reply directly to the person who contributed it without having your reply available for public examination. To reply to the sender, follow these steps.

1. Click Reply to Sender. You'll see the Mail Document window as shown in Figure 4.1. Netscape knows where to send the mail since you are replying to a particular person's message.
2. Click the Subject: field and enter [a subject].
3. Click the Message area and enter [your reply] to the sender.

4. Click Send Mail and you will be returned to the article to which you replied. The message will be sent as mail. This is just like sending mail in Netscape which you learned about in Chapter 4.

Printing an Article

You may want a copy of an article that you have read. You can get one by using the Netscape print option. To print an article, follow these steps:

1. Be sure the article you want to print is active and on the screen.
2. Click File, and then click Print. If you just want to preview the article, click File, then click Print Preview, and you will see a preview of what the article will look like if printed.

Quitting Netscape News

The only way to get out of Netscape news is to go to another Netscape feature. For example, you can click Directory and then click What's Cool to get out of news. You can, of course, always return by clicking the Netscape Back button or even by selecting Go to Newsgroups from the Directory menu once again.

USING NEWSXPRESS FOR NEWS

Netscape news is not the only way to get news. As with other Internet features, there are many different ways to get to the same place. **NewsXpress** is a shareware news reader that offers a more comprehensive set of tools than Netscape and is just as easy to use. It also allows you to see all those thousands of newsgroups so that you can make any selection you want. You don't even have to know the name (such as rec.sport.football.college or alt.tv.spacenuts) first.

Starting and Connecting NewsXpress

To start and connect to NewsXpress, follow these steps. We assume you are no longer in Netscape and are in the group of Windows Internet tools that has been created.

1. Click on the NewsXpress icon . When you do this, you will see the NewsXpress opening window.
2. Click File, amd then click Connect. After you are connected to your INTERNET connection's new site, you will see the connected NewsXpress window as shown in Figure 6.11. When you first sign on to NewsXpress, you will see all the new newsgroups that have become available since your last sign-on that you have not yet had a chance to subscribe to. This list reflects the news administrator's picks. This list of new newsgroups can help you make a decision as to what you might like to subscribe or unsubscribe to.

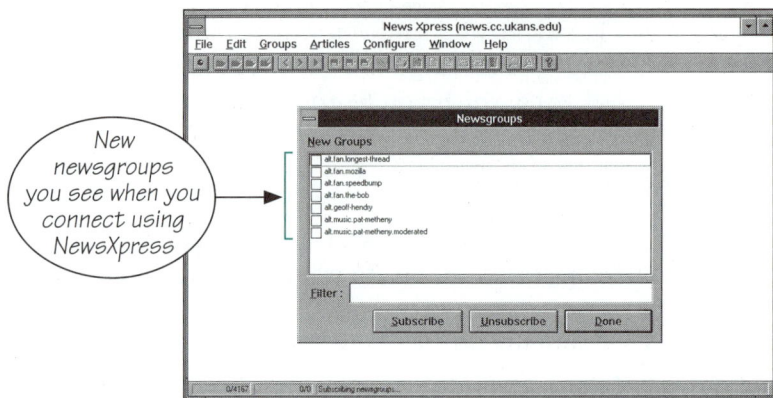

New
newsgroups
you see when you
connect using
NewsXpress

In the NewsXpress opening window you can see elements similar to other
windows you have worked with such as a menu bar and a work area. There's
also a NewsXpress button bar that contains a set of buttons. Click any one of
these and it will perform an operation that is accessible through menu options.
Figure 6.12 shows you what the buttons do. You can easily tell what a button
does by placing the mouse pointer on the button and waiting for a moment.
A small message indicating the purpose of the button will appear as you see
here ⬚⬚⬚⬚. In this section of the chapter we will only cover the most important
of these buttons.

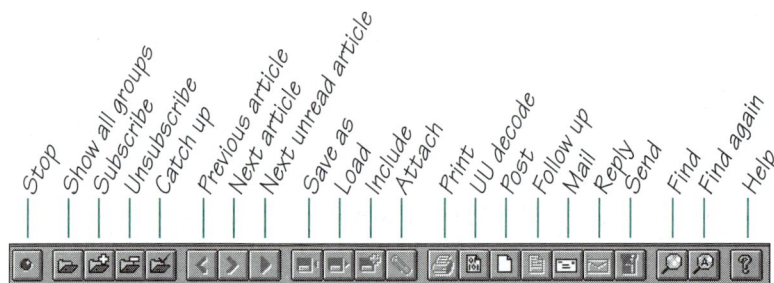

Subscribing and Unsubscribing to Newsgroups

To subscribe and unsubscribe to newsgroups, follow these steps:

1. To subscribe to a newsgroup, click on [the box to the left of the news-
   group] (as you see in Figure 6.11) and click the Subscribe button. You will
   be subscribed to that newsgroup and it will be added to your news file.
   The next time you open NewsXpress, you will see news about that group.

2. To unsubscribe to a newsgroup, click on [the box to the left of the news-
   group] and click the Unsubscribe button. You will be unsubscribed to
   that newsgroup and not see it again, unless it is offered anew.

3. Click Done. As you can see in Figure 6.13, you will be shown the already
   subscribed newsgroups. To the left of the name of each newsgroup is the
   number of unread articles in that group (such as 124 for the newsgroup
   named alt.tv.mst3k).

FIGURE 6.13

The Netscape
window containing
newsgroups already
subscribed to.

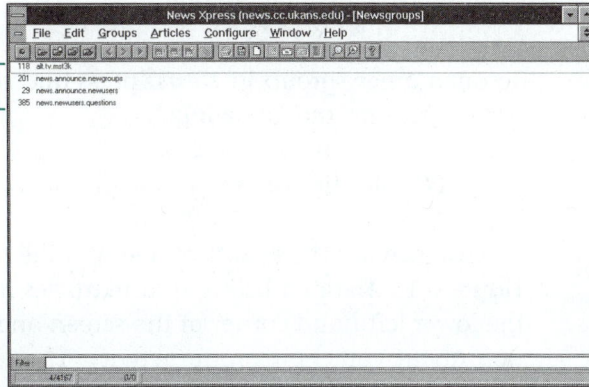

Newsgroups
already
subscribed to

Seeing All the Newsgroups

Now it's time to get started working with groups. Remember earlier in the chapter you read that you can see all the newsgroups that reach your site? Here's how:

> Click Groups, then click Show all Groups. If there is no check next to Show all Groups on the menu, then you will only see those to which you are subscribed. If there is a check (indicating that the Show all Groups option is selected), you will see all the newsgroups available as shown in Figure 6.14.

FIGURE 6.14

All the newsgroups
available at a
news site.

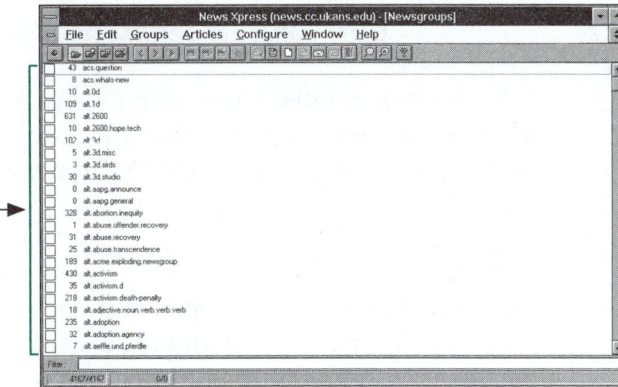

Partial list
of all available
newsgroups

Total
number of
newsgroups

For demonstration purposes, we'll switch back only to the groups that are subscribed to as shown in Figure 6.13.

Opening a Newsgroup in NewsXpress

To open a newsgroup in NewsXpress and see the list of articles in that newsgroup, perform the following:

Double-click on [the name of the newsgroup].

You can see the results of opening the newsgroup named alt.tv.mst3k in
Figure 6.15. Here's a listing of the articles in that group. You can also look at
the lower left-hand corner of the screen and see some numbers with information about your newsgroup activity. The numbers 4/4187 indicate that you
have subscribed to 4 out of 4,187 newsgroups and 123/123 means that all 123
articles in this newsgroup have been read.

FIGURE 6.15

A listing of the
articles in the
mst3k newsgroup.

Articles in
alt.tv.mst3k
newsgroup

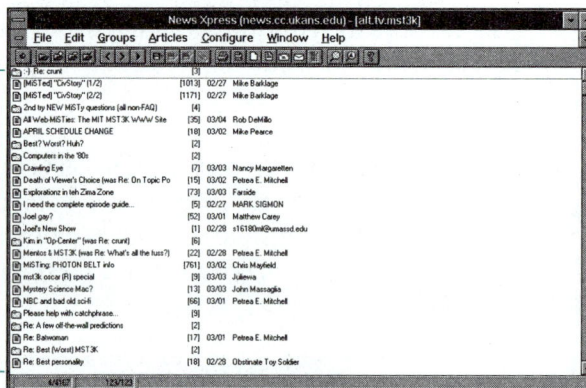

Each article is listed along with the number of lines in the newsgroup, the
date it was created, and the author. For example, Crawling Eye contains 7 lines
and was posted on 3/03 by Nancy Margaretten.

Posting an Article in NewsXpress

Once you have a newsgroup open and can see the listing of articles (as you can
in Figure 6.15), you can post an article which will appear in the listing the next
time the newsgroup is opened. To post an article, follow these steps:

1. Click Articles, and then click Post or press the F5 function key. You will
   see the Post window as shown in Figure 6.16.

FIGURE 6.16
The Post window
where an article
is posted.

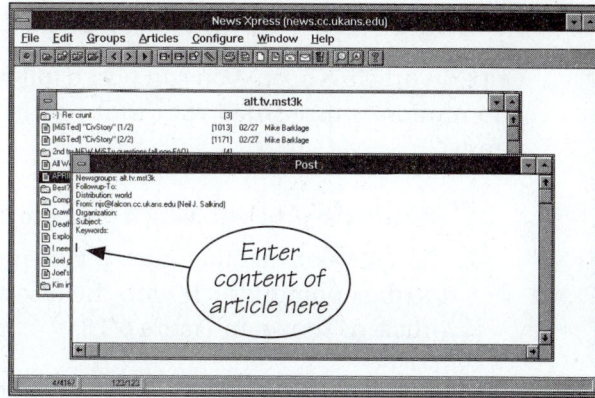

2. Enter [the information you want to appear in the article].

3. Enter [a description] in the Subject: field. Subject is what appears in the list of articles in a newsgroup, so pick a sufficiently descriptive term. You can also enter information about the organization and keywords.

4. Click File, and then click Send55.

5. Click Yes. The next time you start NewsXpress, the article will be posted in the newsgroup along with all the other articles that were previously created.

Reading an Article in NewsXpress

Once you see the articles in a newsgroup, reading one is simple. To read an article using NewsXpress, here's what you do:

Double-click on [the article you want to read]. As you can see in Figure 6.17, there's the article titled "I need the complete episode guide . . ."

FIGURE 6.17
An article in
the alt.tv.mst3k
newsgroup.

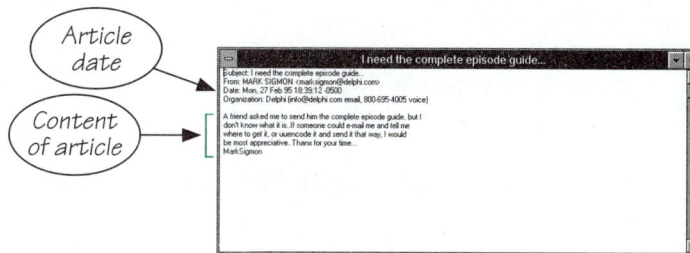

As with Netscape, you can now do various things with this article. You can post a follow-up, reply to it privately, or print it. We'll examine all these options now.

Posting a Follow-Up in NewsXpress

Once an article is open, you can post a follow-up to that article. That way, new information is associated with that article. To post a follow-up, follow these steps:

1. Be sure the article to which you want to post a follow-up is open.
2. Click Articles, and then click Follow-up, or press the F6 function key. You'll see the original article with the insertion point placed at the end of the article as shown in Figure 6.18.

FIGURE 6.18

Posting a follow-up to an article.

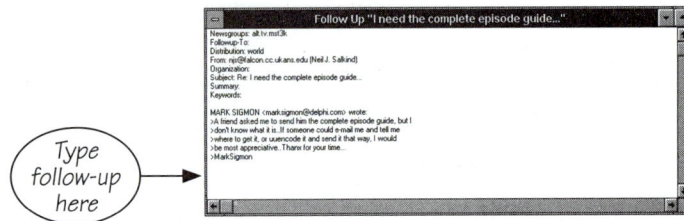

Type follow-up here

3. Type [the information you want included] in the follow-up.
4. Click File, and then click Send.
5. Click Yes. The follow-up will appear as part of that article. Remember, you created a follow-up to an article and not an article itself. It won't appear along with the other articles in the newsgroup.

Mailing an Article

In NewsXpress parlance, this is the same as forwarding an article on to someone else's e-mail address. For example, you might find a particular article especially interesting and want to forward it on to a friend. To mail an article, follow these steps.

1. Click Articles, and then click Mail. You'll see the Mail dialog box as shown in Figure 6.19.

FIGURE 6.19

The Mail dialog box.

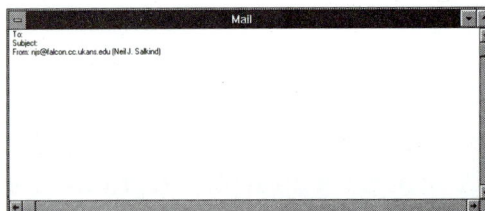

2. Enter [the address to whom you want the article mailed].
3. Click OK.

Replying to an Article

Here's where you want information sent to the individual who created the original document. To reply to an article, follow these steps:

1. Click Articles, and then click Reply. You'll see the article in a Reply dialog box as shown in Figure 6.20, with your name and e-mail address at the top, the content of the article, and the insertion point at the end of the text. Add whatever information you might like at the insertion point.

FIGURE 6.20
The Reply dialog box.

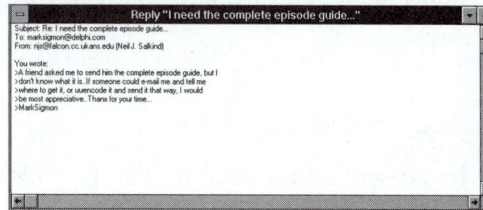

2. Click File, and then click Send. The reply will be sent only to the original author of the article and to no one else.

Printing an Article

Finally, NewsXpress lets you print an article much like you would print any document within a Windows application. To print an article, follow these steps:

1. Be sure that the article you want to print is on the screen.
2. Click File, and then click Print.
3. Click OK. The content of the article, any added follow-ups, or whatever is contained in the article window, will print.

Quitting NewsXpress

Remember that when you are using NewsXpress, you are connected to your Internet connection. To quit NewsXpress, follow this step:

Click File, then click Disconnect.

USING MAILING LISTS

There's another really neat way to use newsgroups. That's when you sign up for a **listserv discussion group**. A listserv discussion group is an automatic depository for information. If you subscribe to it, everything that the list receives, you receive as well. A mail list is also known as a **listserv mailing list**. For example, if you belong to the juggler's mailing list, then each time someone sends mail to that list, you will receive it as well. There are more mail servers than you can imagine, and it will take some exploration to find out which ones fit your needs.

To subscribe to a mailing list, send a message to the administrator of the list. As soon as you do that, a constant stream of messages will come your way. But be careful—if a list is very active, you can receive hundreds of messages in one day. And if you go even a day without checking your mail, it is likely to get so filled with messages that you won't be able to read anything! Imagine your real mailbox outside your apartment or home. When it gets stuffed, it's very difficult to pull out any one piece since everything is jammed in so tightly. You need a bigger mailbox, or you need to empty it before it gets full. Such is the case with a mailing list. Either get a larger e-mail box (ask for more storage space from the system administrator) or check your mail more than once a day.

How to Get on a List

To subscribe to a mailing list, provide the location of the list and a message telling the list administrator you want to subscribe. For example, here are the steps we would use to subscribe to a list containing an ongoing discussion about movies and TV. You need to be in Eudora or some other mailing program.

1. Type listserv@ualvm.bitnet in the To: field. This is the general mail command you learned about in Chapter 3. Notice that a Re: field is not included in the entire mail message.

2. In the message area, type subscribe tv salkind55. Here you enter the word *subscribe* followed by the name of the list and your name.

3. Click Send.

The subscribe message will be sent to the list administrator and you will begin receiving every mail message sent to that site. It's very important that the only thing you enter in the body of your mail message is *subscribe* and whatever other information the list administrator wants. Additional information will confuse the list server since all it expects is *subscribe* or *unsubscribe*. It knows where to subscribe and unsubscribe using your e-mail address.

Some lists have very specific instructions that you'll probably find out about when you discover the list. For example, if you wanted to get all the press releases from the Clinton White House on an automatic basis (without asking for them), you would do the following.

1. Type clinton-info@campaign92.org in the To: field. This command is the e-mail address for the mailing list which contains press releases.

2. Type subscribe clinton-info Neil Salkind in the message section.

3. Click Send. That's it. Before you know it, you'll be receiving all of Mr. and Mrs. Clinton's press releases.

HOW TO
GET ON
A LIST

1. Type [listserve@ followed by the domain name] in the To: field on the e-mail program.

2. Type subscribe as the message.

3. Click Send.

How to Get Off a List

Mailing lists are great, but it can be quite disconcerting when you get thousands of messages and are no longer interested in the Grateful Dead or mass transit. So, you want to unsubscribe. Don't worry. It's as easy as subscribing. Here's how to unsubscribe to the TV and movies list we just subscribed to.

1. Type listserv@ualvm.bitnet in the To: field.

2. Type unsubscribe in the message area.

3. Click Send.

As is the case with subscribing, the list will use your Internet address to complete the operation. If I were no longer interested in receiving Clinton White House press releases, I would enter unsubscribe or please discontinue sending releases or some other message to let them know I am no longer interested in remaining on the list.

A Load of Lists

The names of the list and addresses you see below were taken from a list of over 3,500 lists (that's right—3,500) that go on for some 360 $8\frac{1}{2}$" × 11" pages! This **list of lists**, located at Dartmouth College, consists of the name of the list, topics, who's in charge, and the site address for getting on the mailing list plus some information about the lists. Here's one example from the Dartmouth list. It shows a complete listing, with the name of the list, the address for your subscription request, the person who administers the list, and a description of what the list does.

```
Books antiquaria@aol.com listserv@aol.com Book Dealers Joshua Capy

<JoshuaC2@aol.com>   ANTIQUARIA is a subscription mail list that is
expressly for rare book dealers to exchange information and books
amongst each other and to meet with individuals and institutions
looking for specific books. The list is open to anyone that has
e-mail access to the Internet. The nature of this list is somewhat
unique. First its purpose is to partially fill the gap left by the
demise of Bookquest and second it is an experiment in running a
listserv that is not affiliated with a public institution and is
not on the Internet.
```

In Table 6.3 you can see a list of twenty-five lists on the list (!) to give you some idea of the diversity and richness that mailing lists can bring to your Internet activities.

TABLE 6.3   A list of mail lists.

List Name	Subject
listserv@cunyvm.cuny.ed	Asian American culture
listserv@asuvm.inre.asu.edu	counseling and human development
listserv@ualvm.bitnet	film and tv
listserv@ibm.gwdg.de	archeology
listserv@mizzou1.missouri.edu	journalism in the Baltic countries
listserv@vm.gmd.de	dental amalgam and mercury poisoning
listserv@tritu.bitnet	rock and roll
listserv@bdt.ftpt.ansp.br	biodiversity
listserv@sjuvm.stjohns.edu	disabilities and employment
listserv@ksuvm.ksu.edu	psychology
listserv@pccvm.bitnet	discussion diabetic patients
listserv@utarlvm1.uta.edu	advanced dungeons and dragons discussion
listserv@finhutc.hut.fi	ethology
listserv@cornell.edu	music and recordings of the pre-LP era
listserv@umcvmb.missouri.edu	African American research
listserv@wkuvx1.wku.edu	KISS (the band)
listserv@ksuvm.ksu.edu	Middle Ages sexuality
listserv@miamiu.bitnet	Cincinnati Reds
listserv@uci.com	housing
listserv@allman-request@world.std.com	Allman Brothers Band
listserv@AR-Talk-Request@cygnus.com	Animal Rights
listserv@bikecommute-request@bike2work.eng.sun.com	bike commuting
listserv@obed-l@reepicheep.gcn.uoknor.edu	dog obedience training
listserv@tcsvm	humor
listserv@sjsuvm1.bitnet	air-cooled Volkswagen

You can tell by the general titles what a variety of lists exists—on almost anything you want information about. And all you need do is e-mail the specified location and enter a message telling the list administrator that you want to join. Keep in mind that what you see here is less than one-tenth of 1 percent of what's available. Seek and you shall surely find!

BITNET, a network formed mostly of academic and research institutions also has mail servers galore. Requests to mail servers on BITNET should use the word *listserv* (which stands for list server). As you can see above, all the sample lists taken from the Dartmouth catalog start on BITNET.

NEWSGROUP NETIQUETTE Manners once again count. Only this time, you will be interacting with people in as direct a way as the Internet allows. Be especially conscious of the guidelines in Box 6.1.

BOX 6.1
Guidelines for newsgroup netiquette.

1. When entering a follow-up to a message, try to keep the text short and concise.

2. If you pose a question within a newsgroup, ask that responses come to you by e-mail rather than increasing the number of articles in a group.

3. Be sure that you include your e-mail address, even though it may automatically be included as part of your follow-up message.

4. Don't use other people's articles without proper representation and credit.

5. Subscribe to groups with care, since even the smallest number of subscribed groups will result in hundreds of articles to read.

6. Don't oversubscribe. Go only to those groups that you have use for on a regular basis. You can always add more groups later.

Dear Miss Manners:

There is so much news for me to read that I simply can't handle it all. The prospect of looking through 3,000 newsgroups each day makes me so upset that I want to FLAME the next person who e-mails me anything! Some relief, please!

On-line at dc.foggyb.edu

Dear Gentle News Reader:

Miss Manners assumes that you are new to news [:–)]. You should spend your first few days just getting used to the fact that there is so much to select from. Then, perhaps you can unsubscribe or kill those groups and threads you no longer find useful. Go slowly and work in short chunks of time—both will help.

missmanners@benice.com

There's no place on the Internet that's better to find information than newsgroups. As you have seen here, you can find information about almost any topic, ask questions, and offer solutions. Once you've done your housekeeping and subscribed to those groups you are interested in and are used to the hierarchy of groups, threads, and articles, you'll find yourself working quickly and efficiently through all the news that your site provides.

KEY WORDS

article

follow-up

list of lists

listserv discussion group

listserv mailing list

newbies

newsgroup

news reader

NewsXpress

post

subscribe

thread

unsubscribe

USENET

REVIEW QUESTIONS

1. What is the difference between the main set of newsgroups and the alternative set of newsgroups?

2. What is the name of the Internet tool that allows you to read news at your PC?

3. What is the difference between a newsgroup, a thread, and an article?

4. Why are there usually more articles in a thread than threads in a newsgroup?

5. Why would you unsubscribe to a newsgroup? What happens when you do? And why would you want to subscribe to a newsgroup once you've already unsubscribed?

6. What are the advantages of reading news in Netscape over NewsXpress? News-Xpress over Netscape?

7. When you save a thread, where is the saved file located?

8. What is the danger in subscribing to too many mail lists?

EXPLORATION EXERCISES

1. Start your news reader and identify the first newsgroup in the sci.group (such as sci.animals or sci.astronomy).

2. Call the system administrator at your school and ask how many newsgroups are accessed at this Internet connection. Then ask what criteria are used to decide which groups are selected and which are not.

3. Go to the rec.humor newsgroup and select some funny articles. Now mail them to yourself using your e-mail address.

7

Using Telnet: Remote Control

After this chapter you will be able to

- Understand the telnet command
- Use Netscape and Ewan to telnet to connect to a remote computer
- Identify port numbers to get the service you need
- Telnet to the Library of Congress and use the on-line catalog
- Telnet to Newton, a large bulletin board

In the last chapter, you learned how to read news about topics as diverse as comic books, pasta primavera, and the Saturn Coupe; you also learned how to make your own contributions to newsgroups. Internet news allows you to access information contributed by thousands of Internet users like yourself.

There's another way to get information from the Internet. Through a connection with any one of the thousands of computers on the Net and use of the telnet command, you can sign on to a remote computer site and, as if you were sitting at that computer, use the entire system to which it is connected. For example, you can telnet to the Library of Congress and explore their collection of millions and millions of volumes. Or, you can telnet to the University of Kansas and get an extensive bibliography on Russian history. From your computer, as we will show you in this chapter, you can tap into the vast ocean of information that computers on the Internet have access to. With telnet, you're in control.

WHAT IS TELNET? **Telnet** is an Internet command that allows you to access computers that are interconnected on the Internet. You become a **client** of that computer and the computer is your **host.** Once you're connected, you can use the information at the site much like you use information you access from the computer connection at your college or university. Just as you go to your bookshelf for a reference book, you can go to another computer on the Net.

But, as always with the Internet, the question is where to go to find what you want. There are several lists that provide you with extensive listings of what resources are offered by different telnet sites. One of these lists is the Scott Yanoff list that we mentioned in Chapter 5. Another list that's 1,800 pages long contains a list of telnet sites and a description of what each one contains. The list is available at the ftp site ftp.uwp.edu. The file you want is in the directory /pub/msdos/dir, and the file name is ddir10.zip (for DOS) and wdir.zip (for Windows). You'll notice that the file is compressed and you will need pkunzip (a file commonly available on large ftp sites) to decompress the file.

A Word About Ports

When you telnet to a site, you may have to indicate what **port** you want to use to get the service you want. Not all remote sites require a port address, but some do. For example, to find out the major league baseball schedule, you would telnet to

```
culine.colorado.edu 862
```

where the port address is 862. Other port addresses provide you with schedules for other sports such as hockey or football.

If a telnet site needs a port number and you don't supply it, the site will not recognize your request to sign on. You'll get a message like *Unknown Host*. If you are getting information about a telnet site from a friend or some other resource, be sure that you ask about the appropriate port number, if there is one. You can always try a telnet site without entering the port and it may work. Or it may not. The default port for any telnet site is 23. Use this number following the telnet address as a last resort.

A Word About Terminals

If everything in the computer world were standardized, life would be much easier. But the computer world and the Internet are young and there are still standards that need to be worked out. One standard is the type of **terminal** your connection to the Internet is emulating. When you use the telnet command, however, you will most likely not be asked what type of terminal you are emulating. Fortunately, Netscape and Ewan (the two tools we are using in this chapter) do not require you to specify. Some sites, however, need to know so that the information you get back is readable. The most common terminal emulation is ANSI, or American National Standards Institute. This is especially the case if you are using a PC and the MS-DOS operating system. If you are using Windows as an operating system, the correct terminal emulation is probably VT-100; you should indicate this when asked. If you find that you see all kinds of funny characters on the screen, that terminal emulation may not work and you should try the ANSI.

How will you know when your telnet connection needs terminal emulation information? Somewhere in the set-up or configuration screen, there will be a terminal set-up option. Enter ANSI or VT100 and press Enter. You may be given a list from which to select. Some sites will assume that the type of terminal you are using is a VT-100. Usually, there's a *pick this choice if your terminal is not listed* option. Watch for this if you have no other choices.

Using Netscape and Telnet

Using telnet is very easy. As with other commands in Netscape, you enter the URL in the Open Location box as shown in Figure 7.1. For example, to telnet to the Library of Congress, follow these steps:

FIGURE 7.1
Using Netscape to connect to a remote site.

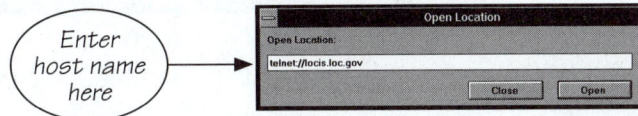

1. Start Netscape.
2. Click File, and then click Open Location.
3. Type telnet://locis.loc.gov and press Enter. You'll then be connected to that remote site. The general form of any telnet command is

   telnet [domain name] [port number]

   which is entered into the Open Location: field.

Two cautionary notes before we begin our telnet tour: First, telnet sites are often difficult to connect to, so don't be surprised if you get a *connection refused* message or something to that effect. Continue to try. Second, Netscape does not have a built-in telnet application—you have to tell Netscape which application you are using. If you are networked and in a computer lab, you probably need not worry about this. If you are configuring Netscape to work with the telnet command, you have to go to the Preferences option on the Options menu in Netscape and indicate which telnet application you are using and where it is located. For the examples in this chapter, we are using Ewan.exe, a simple telnet tool. When you connect through Netscape, you will see the same screens as if you had connected directly through Ewan, so let's go to that application and see what telnet can bring to your Internet world.

USING EWAN   To start Ewan, follow these steps.

1. Click on the Ewan icon 🐿️ EWAN. When you do this, you will see the Ewan opening screen as shown in Figure 7.2. By default, Ewan shows you the list of telnet sites that have already been created and saved. You may see no sites entered in the Connect to Site window as you can see in Figure 7.2.

FIGURE 7.2

The Ewan Connect to site window.

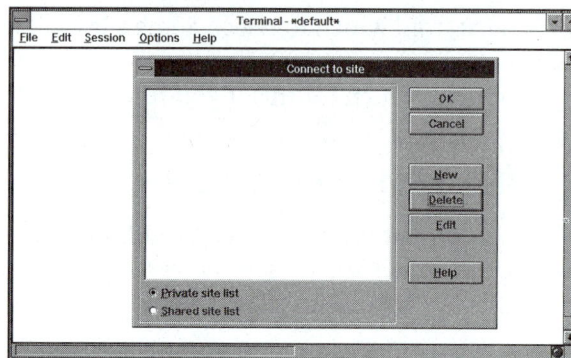

2. Click OK, and you'll see the Ewan opening screen as shown in Figure 7.3.

FIGURE 7.3

The Ewan opening screen.

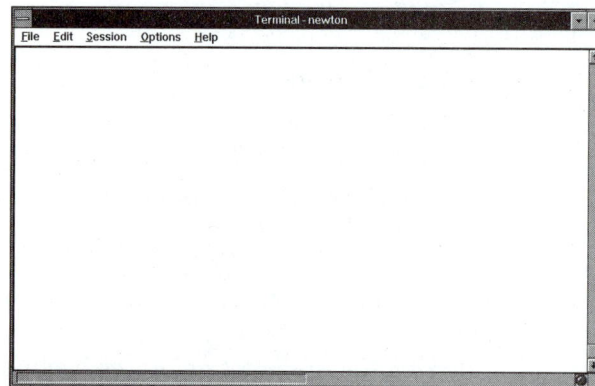

Connecting to a Site

Connecting to a site directly through Ewan requires a few mouse operations. To connect, follow these steps.

1. Click File, and then click Open. When you do this, you'll see the Connect to site window as shown in Figure 7.2.

2. Click New. When you do this, you'll see the Address dialog box shown in Figure 7.4.

FIGURE 7.4
The Address
dialog box.

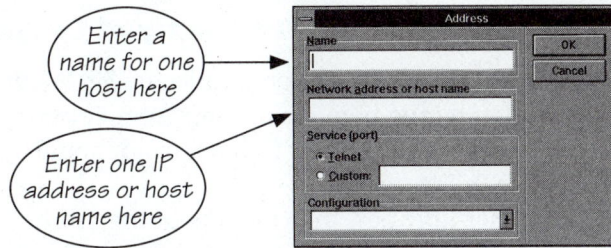

Enter a name for one host here

Enter one IP address or host name here

3. Type Library of Congress in the Name: field.

4. Press Tab.

5. Type locis.loc.gov in the Network address or host name: field, and then click OK.

6. Click Library of Congress.

7. Click OK. The little circle in the lower right-hand corner of the Ewan window will turn from red to green and the message

```
Connection Established
```

will appear in the lower left-hand corner of the Ewan window. Each time you enter a new site, it is recorded and you will see the list of sites when you first open EWAN. You can click on any of these sites to connect. Or, from the opening screen, you can click Session and then click Connect after highlighting the location of the connection.

You should shortly see the Library of Congress opening screen as shown in Figure 7.5.

FIGURE 7.5
The Library of Congress opening screen.

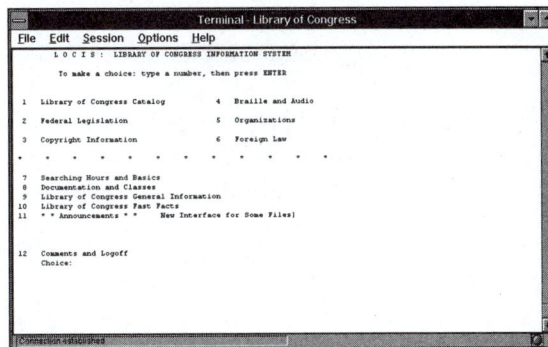

Most telent sites don't require any information when you connect and will provide you with a menu system like the one you see in Figure 7.5. From then on it's a matter of selecting the options you want and working through the windows until you find what you are looking for. Let's take a tour through the catalog of the Library of Congress and get information on an author.

An On-Line Card Catalog: The Library of Congress

We'll begin with the Library of Congress located in Washington, D.C., and look for books written by the popular novelist John Grisham. You should be using Ewan to connect to the Library of Congress and should be in the opening screen we showed you in Figure 7.5.

As with other libraries, the contents of the Library of Congress changes. What you see on your monitor as you complete these steps may not exactly match what you see in the illustrations in this chapter of *Hands-On Internet for Windows*. That should not stop you from going through the exercises as listed since the process described here is exactly what you need to know, regardless of the content of the information.

We want to search through the on-line catalog, which is option #1 in Figure 7.5.

1. Type 1 and press Enter. When you do this, you will see the choices shown in Figure 7.6. Use of the on-line catalog to find out about English language books published after 1968 is option #1.

FIGURE 7.6

Selecting a choice from the on-line catalog at the Library of Congress.

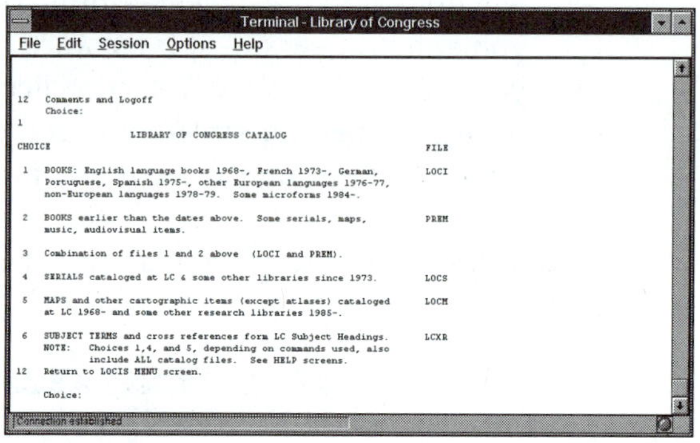

2. Type 1 and press Enter. The Library of Congress will then provide you with a set of commands as shown in Figure 7.7 that allow you to search and browse through the catalog. We want to search for author John Grisham.

FIGURE 7.7

Getting ready to search for an author.

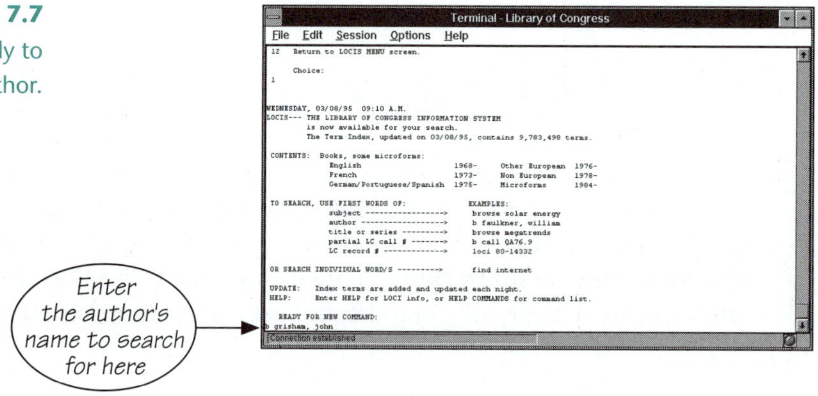

Enter the author's name to search for here

3. Type b grisham, john (as you see in Figure 7.7) and press Enter. The Library of Congress lists authors by their last name (see Figure 7.8) and presents an entire list of those with the last name *grisham*. Instructions to select the author and list his works are at the bottom on the screen.

FIGURE 7.8

The list of authors from which you can select, find, and retrieve information.

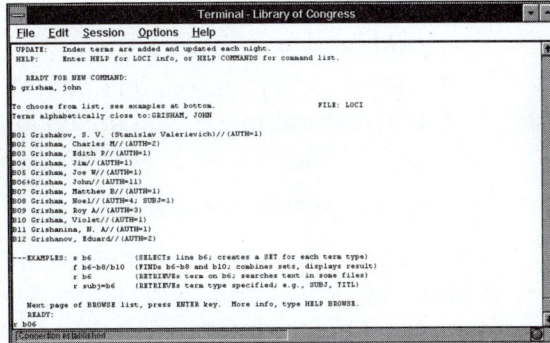

4. Type r b06 (as you see in Figure 7.8) and press Enter. This command retrieves line b06 which contains the information we want about Grisham. Figure 7.9 shows the first screen containing that information.

FIGURE 7.9

The results of the on-line card catalog search.

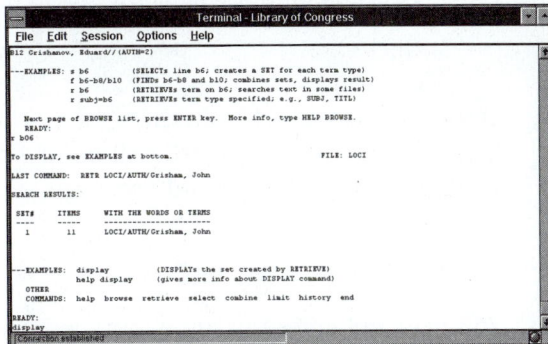

Next, we want to display the items that were retrieved.

5. Type display (as you see in Figure 7.9) and press Enter. Figure 7.10 displays four of the eleven items that the Library has available. If you press the Enter key, you will see the remaining six items on your screen.

FIGURE 7.10

Displaying records from the Library of Congress on-line catalog.

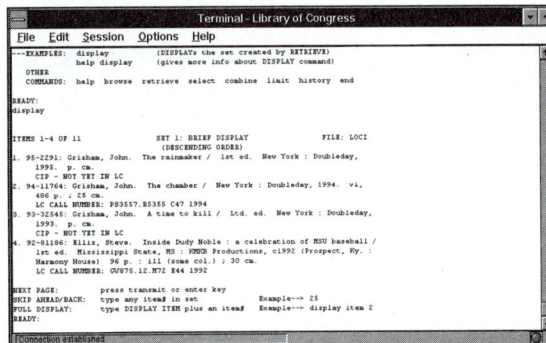

6. Continue to press the Enter key until you reach the end of the information you requested. Once you have reached the end of the set that was being displayed, it's time to disconnect from the Library of Congress.

7. Type quit.

8. Type 12 and press Enter twice to leave the Library of Congress on-line card catalog.

9. In Ewan, click Session, and then click Disconnect. The green light turns to red, showing that you are no longer connected.

Capturing Information in Ewan

As you visit sites, it's likely that you will find valuable information you want to make a record of and consult later. The easiest way to do this is to capture the screens (and the information they contain) as they scroll by and save them as a file. To capture information in Ewan and save it as a file, follow these steps.

1. Click File, and then click Open capture File.

2. Type [a location] and [name] for the file. Everything that passes on the screen will be recorded as part of the file.

3. Click OK.

Once you disconnect from the session, click File, and then click Close capture file. Whatever was captured will be saved as an ASCII or text file and can be read using almost any word processor.

Saving Telnet Sites in Ewan

You need not enter the same telnet address each time you want to visit a site. You can create a file of connections that allow you to go back there with a few clicks. Here's how. You should be in the Ewan opening screen.

1. Click File, amd then click Open. You'll see the Connect to Site dialog box you saw in Figure 7.2.

2. Click New. You'll see the Address dialog box shown in Figure 7.11.

FIGURE 7.11
Need caption.

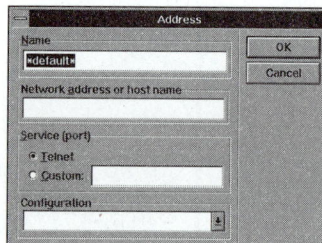

3. Type the name of site in the Name: field.

4. Type the [host name or address] in the Network address or host name field. For example, we entered information about the Library of Congress.

5. Click OK. Once you click OK, you'll see that the site has been added to the Connect to site list.

To connect to any site in the list, follow these steps:

1. Click on [the site].

2. Click OK.

3. Click Session, and then click Connect.

Over time, you will build up a nice list of sites to telnet to. Creating a Connect to site list makes connecting very easy. It also relieves you of having to remember telnet host names which are often cryptic and give no clue as to where they connect.

A Bulletin Board: Newton at Argonne National Laboratory

We just visited the Library of Congress. Now let's look at a bulletin board courtesy of the Argonne National Laboratory, one of the foremost research centers for work in the area of physics. They administer a bulletin board named Newton that you can telnet to and ask questions to scientists, tell someone how to play the addictive computer game Lemmings, or discuss your book collection. Here's how (disconnect from any other telnet sites and go to the opening Ewan screen):

1. Click File.

2. Click New.

3. Type Library of Congress in the Name: field.

4. Press Tab.

5. Type * in the Network address or host name field.

6. Click Session, and then click Connect. The little circle in the lower right-hand corner of the Ewan window will turn from red to green and the message

Connection Established

will appear in the lower left-hand corner of the Ewan window. When you do this, you will be connected to Newton and see the information on your screen shown in Figure 7.12.

FIGURE 7.12
Connecting to
the bulletin board
named Newton.

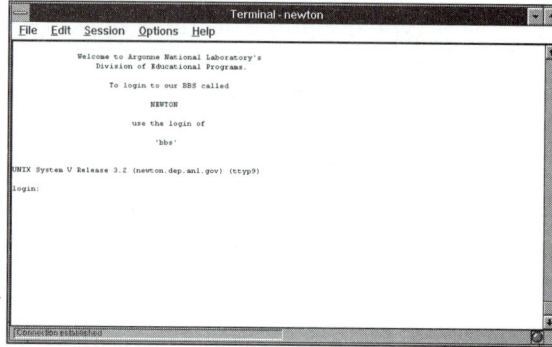

7. At the password prompt, type bbs and press Enter. The next screens you see (starting with the one shown in Figure 7.13) are the Newton welcome screens containing information about the bulletin board as well as messages from the system administrator advising you on changes in the bulletin board and bulletin board policies.

FIGURE 7.13
Information
about Newton.

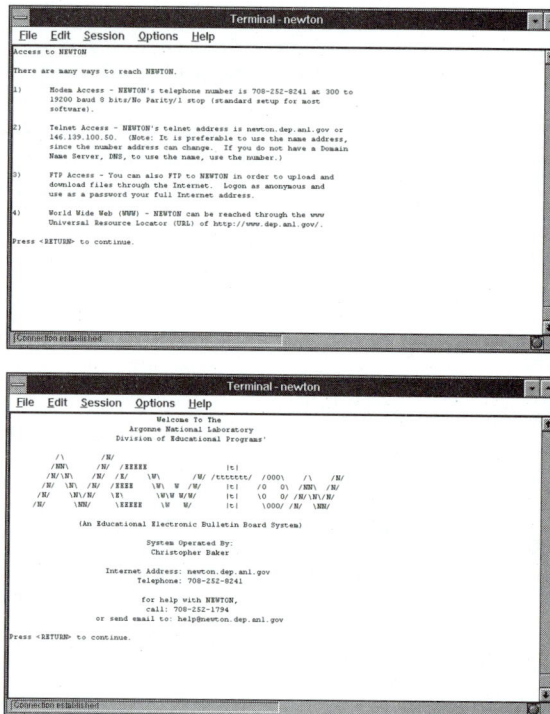

Keep pressing Enter until you have gotten past the welcome, guidelines, and message screens and are asked to enter your sign-on name or enter *new* if you are new. Since you are new, you'll have to provide some information only this one time.

8. Type new and press Enter as you are a new user. The next time you sign on, you will simply have to provide your user id and password.

You'll now start a series of screens that will ask you to register as a new user. You'll need to supply your name, address, phone number, and some other information. This will take about five minutes and is necessary for the system administrator to keep track of who is using the system. Eventually, after you've pressed Enter and have seen lots of screens, you'll get to the [[Main Menu]], as shown in Figure 7.14, providing you with some choices.

FIGURE 7.14

Welcome screen for the Newton bulletin board.

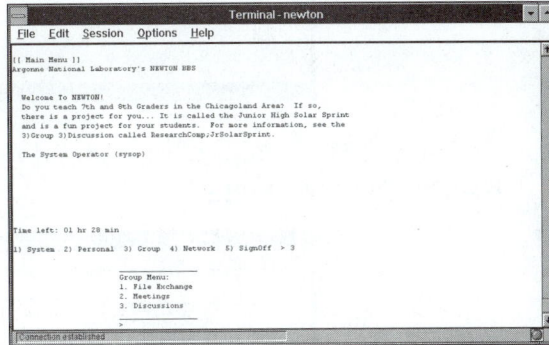

Now we want to explore the discussion groups that are available.

9. Press 3 and Enter to get to the Group menu.

10. Press 3 and then press Enter to enter the Discussions section of the bulletin board. When you do this, you will see a list of 18 available discussion groups as shown in Figure 7.15. We are interested in exploring what the Hobbies discussion group (#9) contains. Keep in mind that what you see in these illustrations may not be identical to what you see on screen. They should be similar enough, however, that you are able to understand the material and what you should do.

FIGURE 7.15

The discussion groups on the Newton bulletin board.

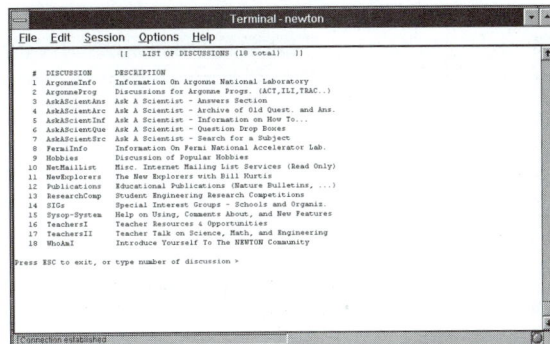

11. Type 9 and press [Enter]. As you can see in Figure 7.16, there are ten topics in the hobbies discussion group. We'll see what's being discussed in the section named Books (#2).

12. Press 2 and press Enter.

FIGURE 7.16
Topics under the
heading Hobbies.

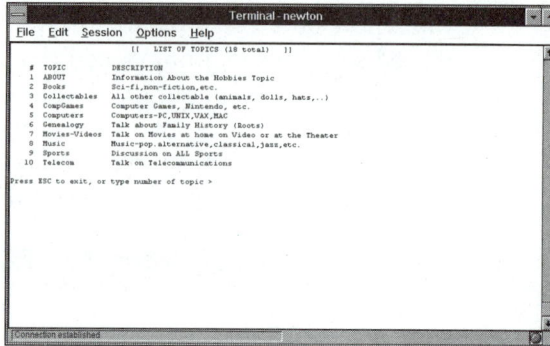

Figure 7.17 contains a list of all the notes made to this Books topic within the general Hobbies group.

FIGURE 7.17
Selecting a
note to read.

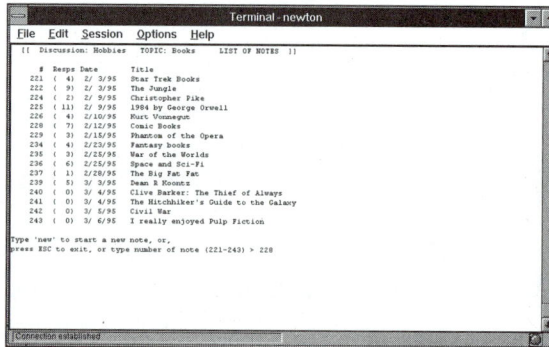

We'll read the notes in discussion #228 on comic books. You can read any one that's available.

14. Type 228 and press Enter. You can see the content of message #227 in Figure 7.18.

FIGURE 7.18
The content
of a note.

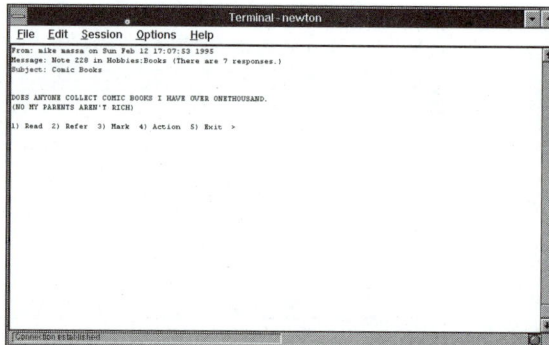

17. Press 5 and press Enter.

18. Press y to confirm that you want to sign off and, as you see in Figure 7.18, you'll be returned to Ewan.

19. Click Special, and then click Disconnect.

A Database: Sports Information

Here we'll telnet to a site that is a database for the major league sport schedules for the National Basketball Association, the National Hockey League, Major League Baseball, and the National Football League. Our example will use port 862 for baseball. You should be in Ewan but not connected to any remote site.

1. Click File.
2. Click New.
3. Type Sports Schedules.
4. Press Tab.
5. Type culine.colorado.edu 862 in The Network address or host name field.
6. Click Session, and then click Connect. The little circle in the lower right-hand corner of the Ewan window will turn from red to green.
7. At the mlb> prompt, type nyy for New York Yankees and press Enter. This produces the schedule of the upcoming games for the New York Yankees as shown in Figure 7.19.

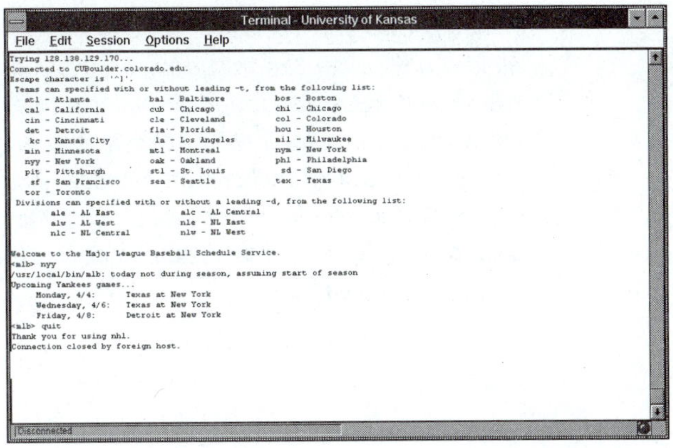

FIGURE 7.19
Upcoming games for the Yankees.

8. Click Special, and then click Disconnect.

In general, telnet is fairly simple to use although using it within Netscape or within a Windows environment in general can be problematic. Check with your instructor or system administrator if you have trouble.

TELNET NETIQUETTE You don't directly interact with people using telnet, as you might using e-mail, but there are some things you need to remember to remain a good Internet citizen. You can see the few, but important, telnet etiquette guidelines in Box 7.1.

BOX 7.1
Telnet netiquette

1. If you don't know what a telnet site offers, then download the readme file which will tell you what's available and how you can get it. Otherwise, you stay on-line, occupying a space that some one else could use to connect.

2. To save space on your Internet connection, always download any information you take from a telnet site to your personal computer and delete the file from the Internet connection.

3. Keep in mind that you are a guest at a telnet site. Be courteous, don't stay on longer than necessary, and obey any rules that the system administrator at the site asks you to read and keep in mind.

4. When requested, supply your user ID. This helps the system administrator keep track of who is using the machine, what site you come from, and other important information that can improve the operation of the Net for everyone.

Telnet allows you to travel around the world and figuratively sit down at almost any computer on the Internet and access that computer's resources. Whether it be a database or bulletin board, you can use telnet to obtain information, interact with others, and search vast resources such as libraries containing millions of volumes. And best of all, telnet might be the easiest of all the Internet skills that you have so far mastered. Just the telnet command and the remote computer's Internet address are all you really need to know.

KEY WORDS

client
host
port

telnet
terminal

REVIEW QUESTIONS

1. How is telnet like other Internet tools such as e-mail?
2. What is the difference between a client and a host?
3. What is meant by the term "remote computer"?
4. What command do you need to enter in order to use telnet through Netscape?
5. What is the relationship between Netscape and Ewan?

EXPLORATION EXERCISES

1. Telnet to `downwind.sprl.umich.edu 3000` and find out what the forecast for Redding, California, is.
2. Telnet to `debra.doc.ca`, use the login `chat`, and talk with a dragon.
3. Telnet to `fedworld.doc.gov` and find out how many minutes you are allowed on this fun and informative site per day.
4. Telnet to `selway.umt.edu`, login as `health`, and find out what's new this month.
5. Telnet to `yfn2.ysu.edu` and find out what special interest groups (or SIGS) are available in the Public Square. What is the first option in the Book SIG?

8

Using Internet Utilities

After completing this chapter, you'll be able to

- Browse the Internet using gopher
- Search for documents using WAIS
- Use Archie to find programs
- Use Veronica to search for words in gopherspace
- Search for documents using WAIS
- Use Netscape White Pages
- Find the e-mail addresses of your friends

Every month, Rick Gates, a very clever librarian at the University of Arizona, begins a contest that hundreds of people all over the world participate in. The goal? To complete the Internet Hunt, ten questions on everything from *Alice in Wonderland* to the upcoming photography exhibit at the California Museum of Photography. The prize? Some signed books, subscriptions, and other goodies—but mostly the fun of using the Internet to hunt down the most esoteric and seemingly unimportant bits of information. And the way Internet users start out finding these answers is through the set of Internet utilities you'll learn about in this chapter.

So far in *Hands-On Internet for Windows*, you have learned about sending e-mail, transferring files, reading news, and remotely connecting and using other computers. In this chapter you'll look at such utilities as Gopher, Archie, Veronica, WAIS, and WHOIS. This chapter is all about finding things on the net. In Table 8.1, you can see a comparison of these different utilities including what they do and how you get to them. The **WWW** (**World Wide Web**) and the browsers available to use with it are utilities as well, and we covered Netscape, one of the best, in Chapter 3.

TABLE 8.1 Internet utilities and what they do.

Utility	What it does	How to get to it
gopher	A menu-driven utility that connects you to different Internet resources by connecting you to those resources.	Use a gopher client to connect to a gopher server or telnet to a gopher server.
Archie	Finds files by searching for specific keywords and also tells you the location of the files.	Use an Archie client on your own machine, or telnet to an Archie server.
Veronica	A menu-driven gopher service that allows you to do keyword searches of gopher menus.	Use a gopher client to connect to a gopher server and then select the Veronica menu items.
WAIS	Searches databases on the Internet using keywords.	Use a WAIS client to connect to the WAIS or telnet to a WAIS server.
WWW	A hypermedia system that retrieves information on the Internet.	Use a WWW client to connect to the WWW or telnet to a WWW server.
WHOIS	A utility for finding out information about Internet users.	Use the WHOIS command at the system prompt.

Throughout this chapter, keep in mind that the Internet is a dynamic entity. It is always changing and some of the screens used to illustrate how these utilities work may not be the ones you see on your monitor. They should, however, be similar enough that you get the idea of how these utilities work and how you can use them. Also keep in mind that the Net is busier today than it was yesterday and will be busier tomorrow than it is today. If you can't connect, try again and always look for another site to connect to that may provide you with the same information.

BROWSING THE INTERNET: USING GOPHER

Gopher is a utility that allows you to search thousands of Internet sites using an easy-to-use menu system. A **gopher client** is the software that you use to access a **gopher server**, which is the index that contains the information about where things are located.

Why the name gopher? For three reasons. First, the word *gopher* is often used as a description of a person who will "go for" something. Indeed, gopher clients and servers work together to go for all kinds of things from weather reports to recipes to jokes. Second, gophers are cute little animals that burrow through tunnels exploring uncharted areas. That's what it will do for you: explore the Internet and find things quickly and easily. Finally, the Golden Gopher is the mascot of the University of Minnesota. Not by coincidence, that's where Gopher was born in 1991.

Surveying Gopherspace Using Netscape

There are two ways you can get to a gopher server and explore **gopherspace**, the thousands of files that gophers can direct you to. The first way is through the use of a gopher client. The second is through telnet. The results will be the same in both cases. The only difference is that using a gopher client is faster since it's a more direct connection.

The general command for using a gopher in Netscape is to enter the following command at the location prompt.

```
gopher:// [server name]
```

For example, the grandparent of all gopher sites is at the University of Minnesota. To connect, we would enter

```
gopher://consultant.micro.umn.edu
```

The general command for using telnet to connect to a gopher server is to type

```
telnet:// [server name]
```

at the system prompt and then enter gopher as the login. For example, to telnet to the University of Minnesota gopher server, we would enter

```
telnet://consultant.micro.umn.edu
```

You can use the telnet tools we talked about in Chapter 7 and go gophering that way. In Table 8.2 you can see a listing of major gopher sites including the host name, IP address, login, and location. You can use any of these. For our illustration here, we'll go to the gopher site gopher.sunet.se, a popular gopher site in Sweden. You should be in Netscape.

TABLE 8.2   Primary gopher sites.

Host	IP Number	Login	Location
consultant.micro.umn.edu	134.84.132.4	gopher	University of Minnesota
gopher.chalmers.se	129.16.221.40	gopher	Sweden
gopher.sunet.se	192.36.125.10	gopher	Sweden
gopher.uiuc.edu	128.174.33.160	gopher	University of Illinois
hafnhaf.micro.umn.edu	134.84.132.4	gopher	University of Minnesota
info.anu.edu.au	150.203.84.20	info	Australia
library.wustl.edu	128.252.173.4	no log in required	Washington University
panda.uiowa.edu	128.255.40.201	panda	University of Iowa
pinto.isca.uiowa.edu	128.255.200.5	gopher	University of Iowa
toten.ouc.cl	146.155.1.16	gopher	Chile
ux1.cso.uiuc.edu	128.174.5.59	gopher	University of Illinois

1. Click File, and then click Open Location.

2. Type gopher://gopher.sunet.se.

3. Click Open. Once the connection is made, you will see the Gopher Menu shown in Figure 8.1.

FIGURE 8.1

Making the gopher connection at sunet.se.

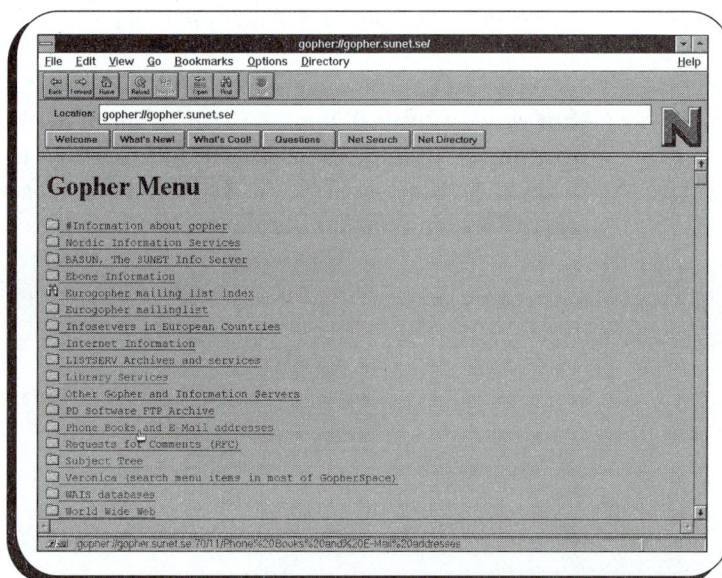

You can see all the options that are available. It's well worth your while to take some time to explore these different options—there's no substitute for direct experience.

Gopher tools can be used to find information about almost anything including finding e-mail addresses for people. We'll look for the e-mail address of a friend at Yale University.

4. Click Phone Books and E-Mail addresses. You'll see a new Gopher menu as shown in Figure 8.2.

FIGURE 8.2

A listing of phone and e-mail addresses available at the sunet gopher site.

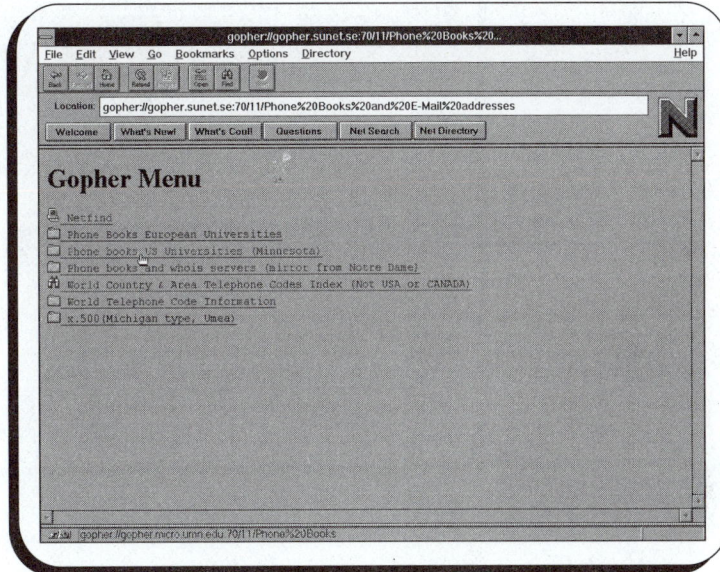

5. Click Phone books US Universities (Minnesota). You'll see a new Gopher menu as shown in Figure 8.3.

FIGURE 8.3

Additional gopher sites containing phone books and e-mail addresses.

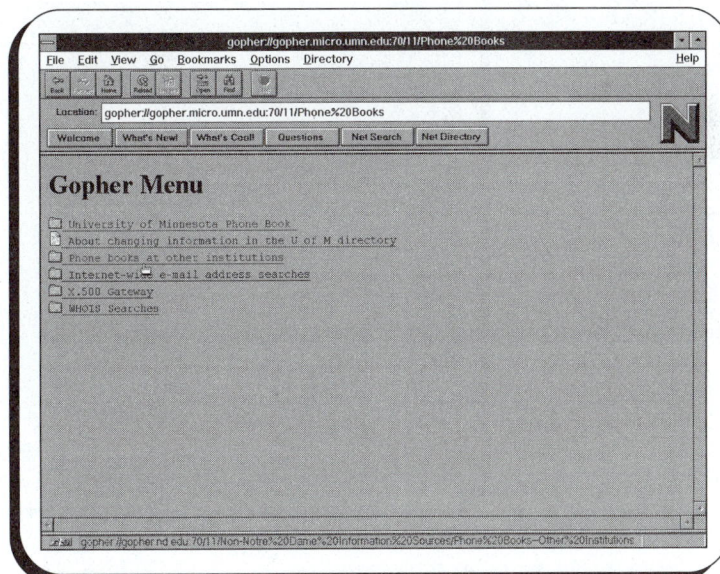

6. Click Phone books at other institutions. Now, as shown in Figure 8.4, you should see a list of possible gopher sites organized geographically. We're looking for Yale University's phone book.

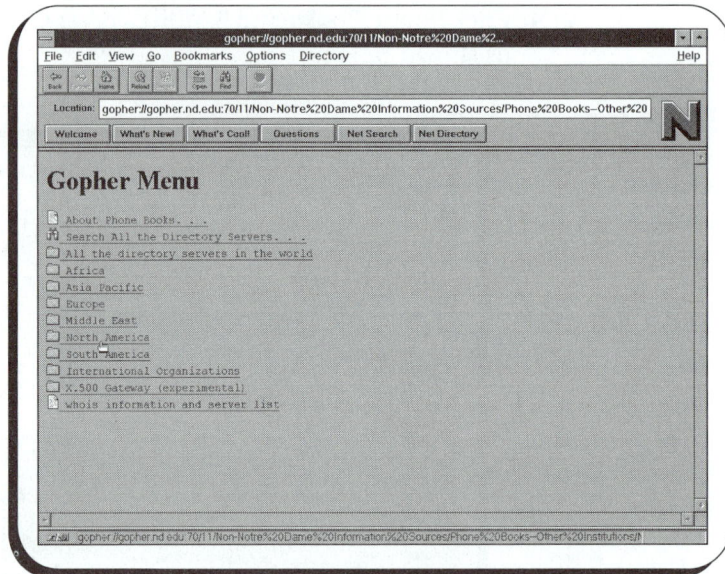

7. Click North America. Figure 8.5 shows a partial listing of all the other institutions available through this gopher site. Scroll down to Yale University.

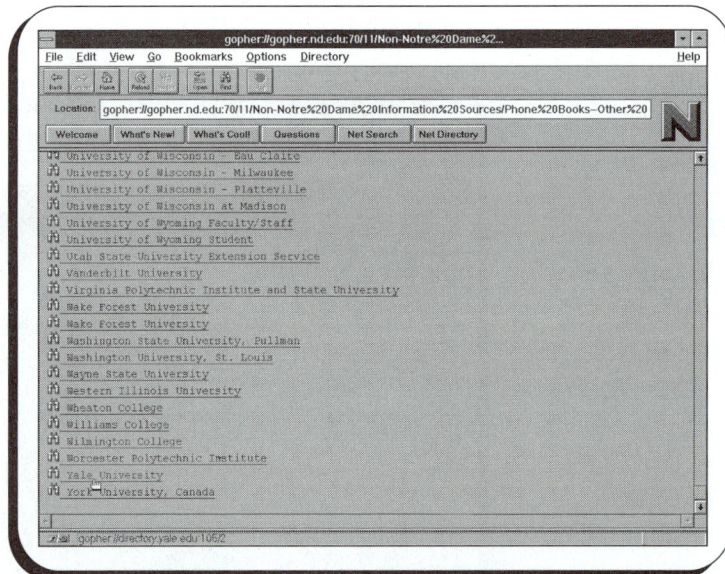

8. Click Yale University.

9. Click in the Enter search keywords: field and type Kirsten Magnuson as you see in Figure 8.6. This is the name of the friend whose e-mail address we are trying to locate.

FIGURE 8.6

Searching for Kirsten at the Yale site.

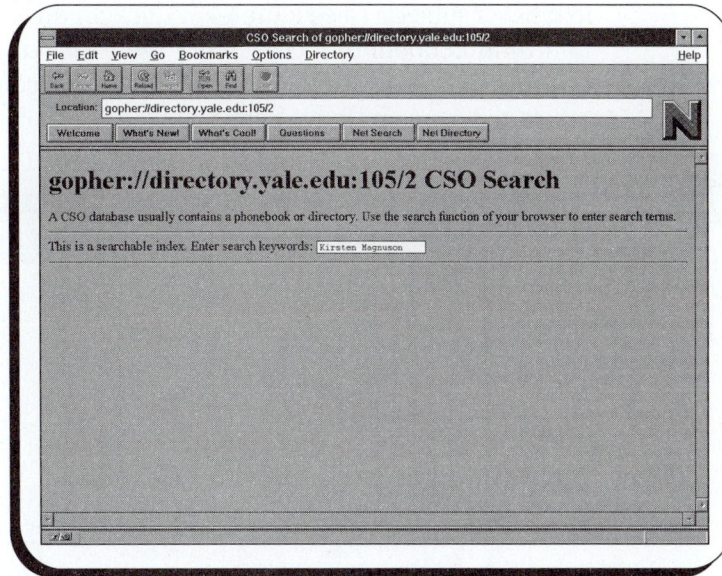

Once the gopher completes its task, you'll see the results as shown in Figure 8.7. Keep in mind that the search could have failed for numerous reasons. Kirsten might not have her e-mail address registered at the Yale site (for whatever reason) or might not have an e-mail address in the first place. Also, the site might be too busy for you to go hunting. If you don't find an address gophering, it only means that you have had no success, not that the e-mail address does not exist or that the person attached to it does not have an e-mail address.

FIGURE 8.7

A successful search and an e-mail address.

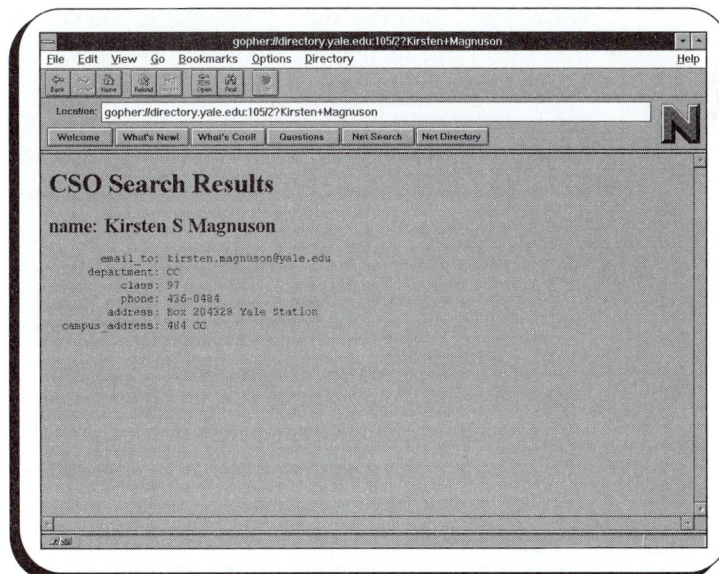

Tons of Other Stuff Through Gopher

We just touched on what you can access through gopherspace. If you click Subject Tree in the opening gopher screen (see Figure 8.1), you will be taken to a list of subjects (see Figure 8.8). Click on any subject to be taken, in turn, to information about that area. Since there's usually more information that you can deal with in any one sitting, be ready to create bookmarks so that you can return to where you have been.

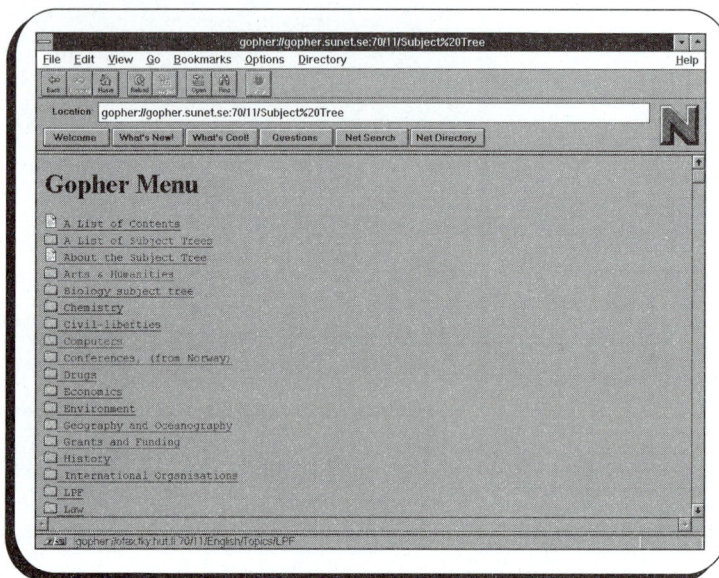

Finding Programs: Using Archie

In Chapter 5 you learned how easy it is to download a file from the Internet to your Internet connection. From there you can download it to your own computer and use as needed. As an illustration, the inet.services.txt (Yanoff list) was downloaded. Even though there are thousands of programs available on the Internet, you can't download any of them unless you can find it. One way to find out where a program or a file is located is to keep your eyes and ears open. Listen to other Internet users, read about new programs, and keep in touch with people on the Net.

There's another way that's easier. **Archie** is the Internet utility that helps you search for and find files. How does Archie work? It regularly searches ftp sites and creates an index of the files that are available. When you request the location of a file, Archie goes into its index and performs the search. Archie is very heavily used during the day—it's not unusual for all Archie sites, especially those in the United States, to be busy. If you can, do your Archie work during the evening hours; searches will be completed much faster. You can find a list of Archie sites in Table 8.3. As you can see, each site is accompanied by a suggested user location. It's best if you stick close to home as searches to faraway Archie sites take up more time and resources on the Net.

TABLE 8.3   Archie sites.

Archie	IP Address	Location
archie.ans.net	147.225.1.10	USA
archie.au	139.130.4.6	Australia
archie.doc.ic.ac.uk	146.169.11.3	United Kingdom
archie.edvz.uni-linz.ac.at	140.78.3.8	Austria
archie.funet.fi	128.214.6.102	Finnland
archie.internic.net	198.49.45.10	USA
archie.kr	128.134.1.1	Korea
archie.kuis.kyoto-u.ac.jp	130.54.20.1	Japan
archie.luth.se	130.240.18.4	Sweden
archie.ncu.edu.tw	140.115.19.24	Taiwan
archie.nz	130.195.9.4	New Zealand
archie.rediris.es	130.206.1.2	Spain
archie.rutgers.edu	128.6.18.15	USA
archie.sogang.ac.kr	163.239.1.11	Korea
archie.sura.net	128.167.254.195	USA
archie.sura.net1526	128.167.254.195	USA
archie.switch.ch	130.59.1.40	Switzewrland
archie.th-darmstadt.de	130.83.22.60	Germany
archie.unipi.it	131.114.21.10	Italy
archie.univie.ac.at	131.130.1.23	Austria
archie.unl.edu	129.93.1.14	USA
archie.uqam.ca	132.208.250.10	Canada
archie.wide.ad.jp	133.4.3.6	Japan

Let's use Archie here to find pkzip.exe, a popular file compression program. As with gophers and other Internet utilities, there are many different Archie tools you can use. We'll use a popular Archie search tool named ArchiePlex-Form, accessible within Netscape, to carry out our search. You should be in Netscape when you begin this exercise.

1. Click Directory (on the Netscape main menu), and then click Internet Search.

2. Scroll down until you find ArchiePlexForm.

3. Click ArchiePlexForm. As shown in Figures 8.9 and 8.10, you'll see a form asking for information about the name of the program you want to search for.

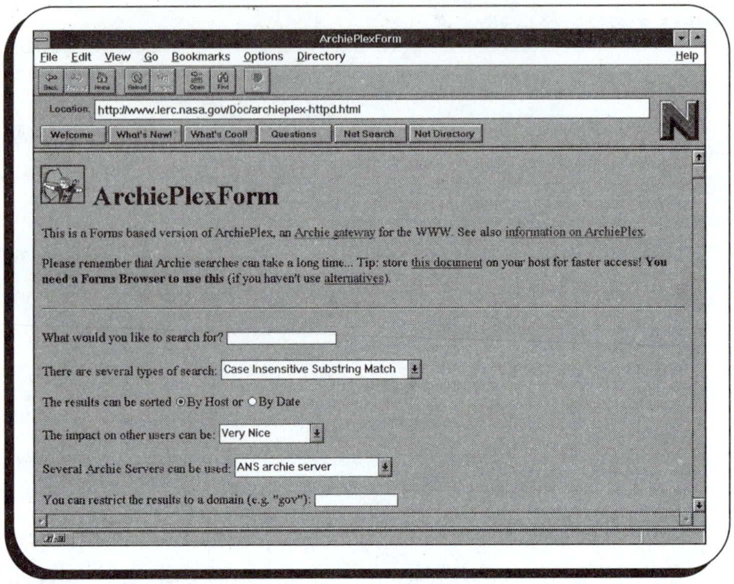

FIGURE 8.9

The ArchiePlexForm form for searching for a filename.

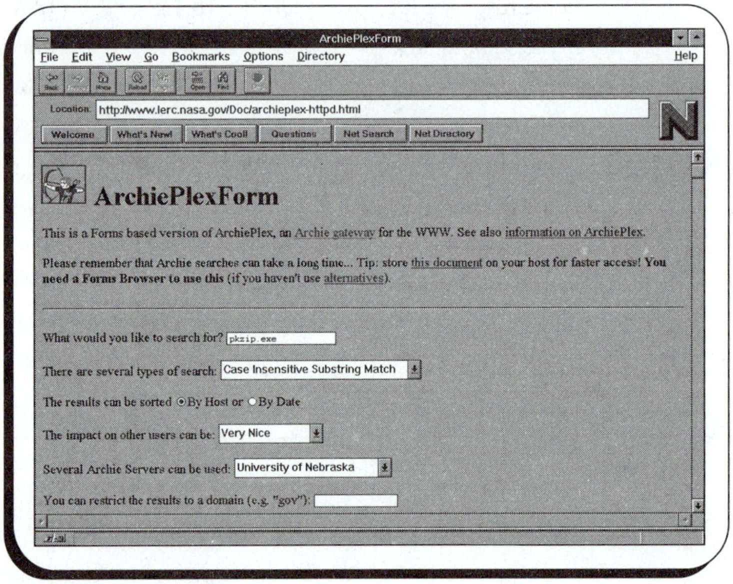

FIGURE 8.10

Entering terms to search for using ArchiePlex.

4. Click in the What would you like to search for? field and type pkzip.exe. The rest of the fields are used to set a variety of parameters for the search. For example, you can click on the field titled You can restrict the number of results (default 95): and enter 10 or 20 (or whatever you choose) to restrict the number of sites ArchiePlex finds with sites that have the file you are searching for. You can also restrict where you search by using the Several Archie servers... field. Experiment with all of these as you work with Archie.

5. Click Submit. Archie searches sites for the program name you specified and comes back with a list of places where the program can be found. This can't be made a lot easier! Check the results of the search in Figure 8.11 which lists sites where pkzip.exe can be found. All it takes now is a simple ftp to that location to get the file.

FIGURE 8.11
The results of the Archie search.

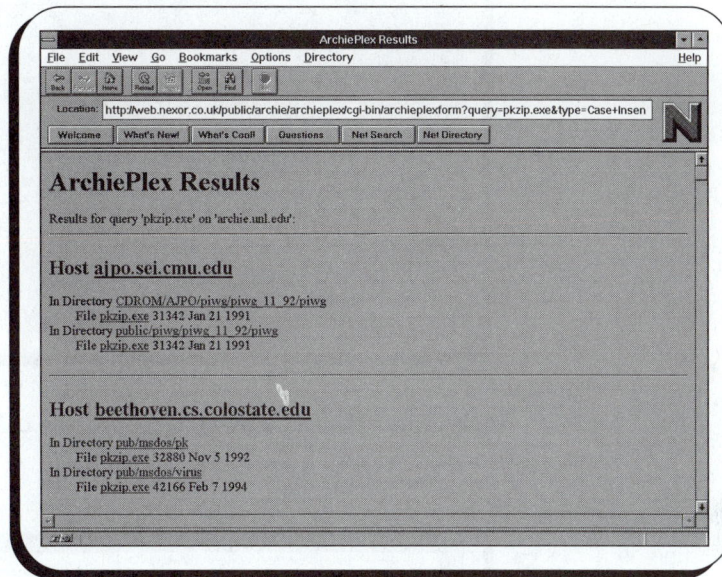

If you want the file you were searching for (pkzip.exe), just click on the name and save it to your hard disk. Simple? Yes!

Searching for Words in Gopherspace: Using Veronica

If you read comics when you were younger or still do, you may remember that Veronica was Archie's heartthrob. Betty was always around when Archie needed a date, but it was Veronica for whom Archie's bell tolled.

Veronica, an acronym for **Very Easy Rodent-Oriented Net-Wide Index to Computerized Archives**, searches for key words among menus in gopherspace. Let's use Veronica to search for pkzip.exe. Since Veronica is a part of a gopher site, we'll first have to sign on to a gopher site as we did earlier. Be sure that you are in an active Netscape screen.

1. Click File, then click Open, type gopher://gopher.sunet.se, and then press Enter. You'll be connected to the gopher site.

2. Scroll down the list on the gopher menu and click Veronica (search menu items in most of gopherspace). In Figure 8.12, you'll see a listing of gopher locations where Veronica is used as the search tool.

FIGURE 8.12

Using Veronica
to search for
key words.

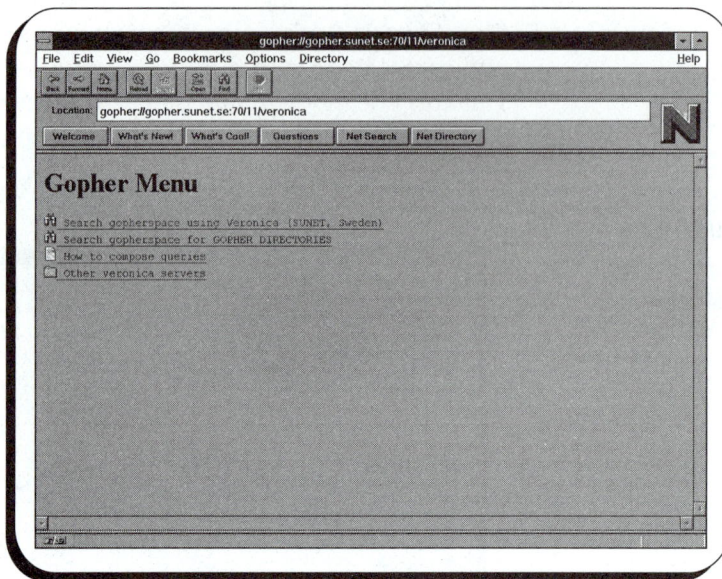

3. Click Other Veronica servers. You'll see a listing of Veronica servers as shown in Figure 8.13.

FIGURE 8.13

A listing of
Veronica servers.

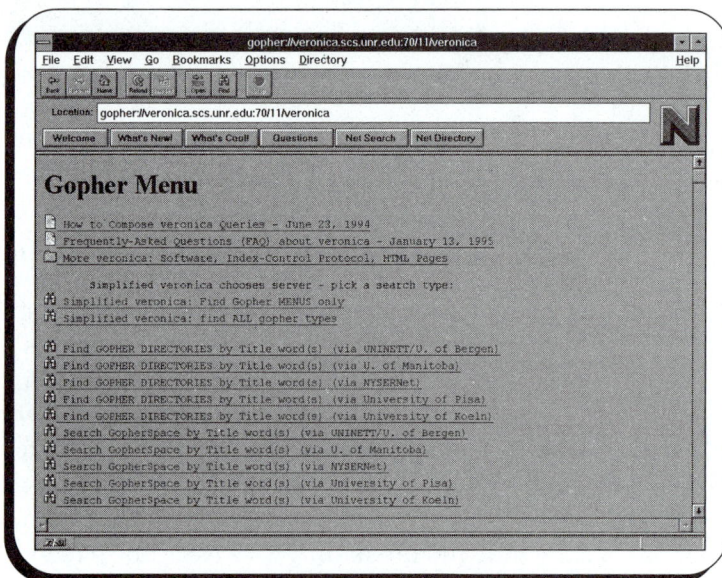

4. Click simplified Veronica: find All gopher types. In Figure 8.14, you see the form for entering the words you want to search for.

5. Type pkzip.exe in the Enter search keywords: field and press Enter.

FIGURE 8.14
A Veronica form
for searching.

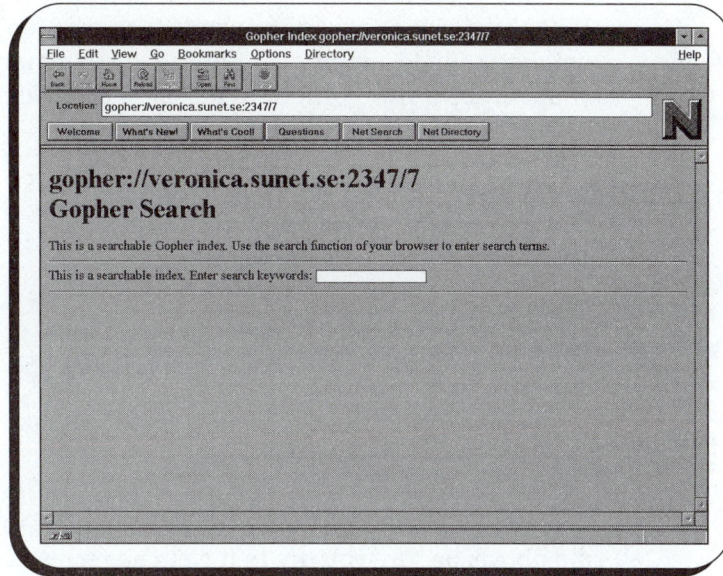

FIGURE 8.14
A Veronica form
for searching.

Veronica does its job and returns with a list of files (see Figure 8.15) that you can download by clicking once on the name and specifying a path where you want the downloaded files to be located.

FIGURE 8.15
The results of a
Veronica search.

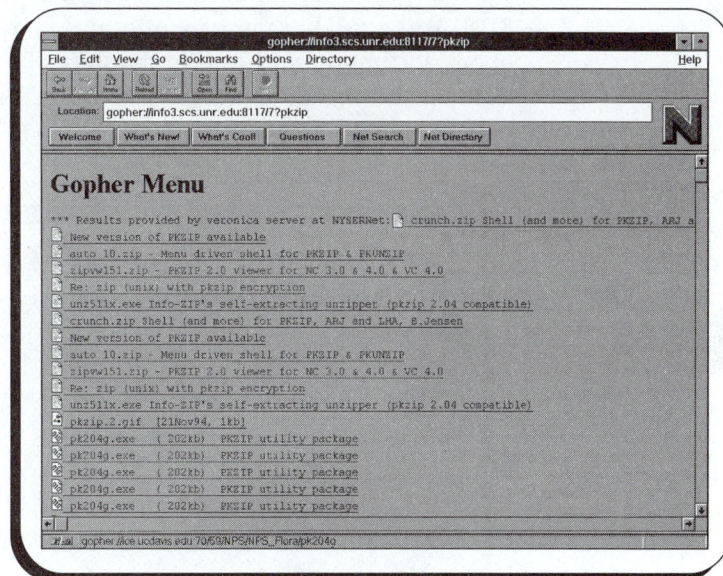

SEARCHING FOR DOCUMENTS: USING WAIS

Archie and Veronica both do a very good job of searching indexes of ftp sites and gopherspace but they don't give you access to the contents of documents within databases. That's what **WAIS**, **Wide Area Information Server**, does.

When you give it a word or words to search for, it searches through Internet databases for documents containing the search words you specify. In Table 8.4 you can see a list of public WAIS sites, also called **SWAIS** for **Simple Wide Area Information Server**.

TABLE 8.4   SWAIS sites.

SWAIS Site Address	How to Log In
hub.nnsc.nsf.net	wais
kudzu.cnidr.org	wais
quake.think.com	wais
sunsite.unc.edu	swais

We'll gopher to a WAIS site and search for the same file, pkzip.exe, as we did above. Be sure you are in a Netscape screen.

1. Click File, click Open, then type gopher://gopher.sunet.se, and then press Enter. You'll be connected to the gopher site.
2. Scroll down the list on the gopher menu and click WAIS databases. You'll see a list of WAIS databases organized by subject as shown in Figure 8.16. You can click on any one and be given extensive information about documents within that database. From there you can continue to click to find the information you want, being more specific with each click as the focus narrows.

FIGURE 8.16

A list of subjects linked to database.

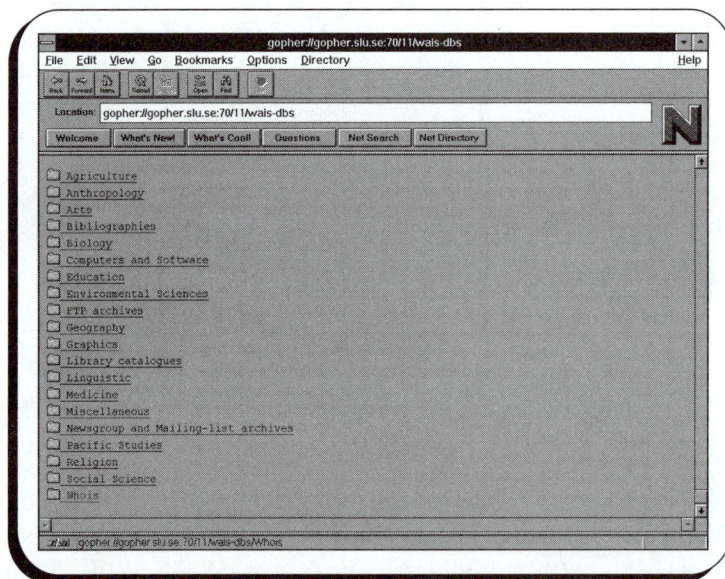

**FINDING
A FRIEND
ON THE NET**

Maybe the most common question people who are new to the Net ask is, "I have this friend in Florida. How can I find his e-mail address?" That's a big question with several different answers. The most obvious is to call the person or send a U.S. mail letter asking your questions. It's a surefire way to get an answer. Beyond that, the Internet includes a bunch of different utilities including programs and files to help you find addresses. While these tools help you find e-mail addresses, a side benefit is that you can use these tools to find people you are trying to locate. You'll see how that can be done later in this chapter. In this last part of the chapter, we'll explore different ways of finding addresses. While you might hit gold with one of them, it's likely that you will have to use more than two of these sources to get the information you want.

Getting College Addresses

There's a newsgroup (see Chapter 6) named soc.college that contains tons of information on colleges and their addresses. Use your news reader to open the newsgroup and then search for information about the particular school you may be interested in. If there is no information, post a follow-up or create a new entry that asks your questions.

For example, a recent review of this newsgroup revealed that people were looking for the e-mail addresses of Purdue University (@purdue.edu) and Indiana University (@indiana.edu). When you get to the university you want, you can then take a shot and enter your friend's first and last name, initials, or some combination to see if you can reach him or her. You might also want to look into the soc.net-people newsgroup for people who are always searching for other people.

Writing the Postmaster

Usually, at every site there is a postmaster who can be of some help to you in your efforts to find addresses. You can address mail to that person as

```
postmaster@domain name
```

(such as postmaster@falcon.cc.ukans.edu) and enter a question such as "I'm trying to find the e-mail address of a person named Doug Springer. Can you please help?" Postmasters are very busy people but will probably not mind if you send a quick note asking for help. But they are not the white pages and do not want to be bothered. Just make a short request and be polite. If there's anything to be found, this person can probably come up with it.

Using WHOIS

WHOIS is an Internet tool that helps you search through a special database of recorded e-mail addresses and provides you with full names and addresses. This is a great tool, but the one drawback is that only registered names will appear. You can get to WHOIS through a gopher server as you see in Figure 8.3. Once you click, you'll be provided with a form. Enter as much information as you can and press Enter. WHOIS will take it from there and try to locate the e-mail address of the person you are looking for.

Using the (Other) White Pages

You've used the phone book to look up a phone number of a friend in the white pages, right? Well, here's the Internet White Pages where you can find just about anything you need. You just have to look. Let's use Netfind and go through the steps of trying to find the e-mail address of a friend we know who has a faculty position at the University of North Carolina.

1. Click Directory (on the Netscape menu bar), then click Internet White Pages, and then click Netfind. The Internet White Pages window will open as you see in Figure 8.17.

FIGURE 8.17

The Internet White Pages.

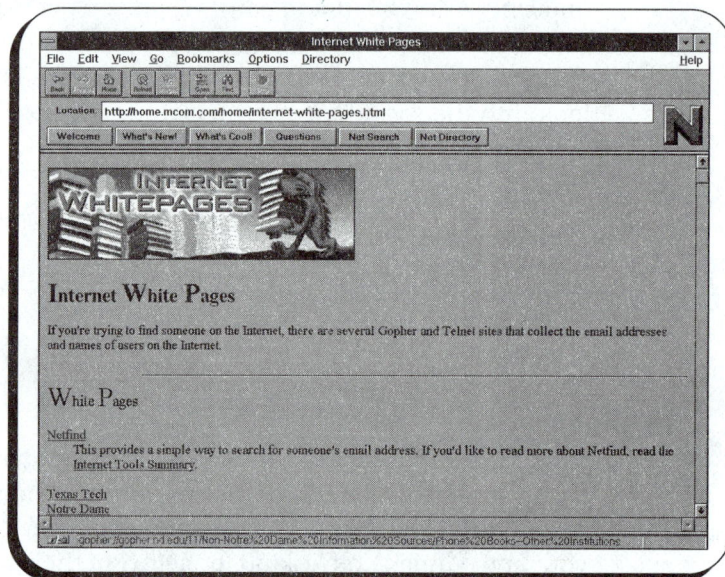

2. Click this as you see in Figure 8.18. It's a good idea to read the contents of this screen so you can get some basic instructions on using Netfind.

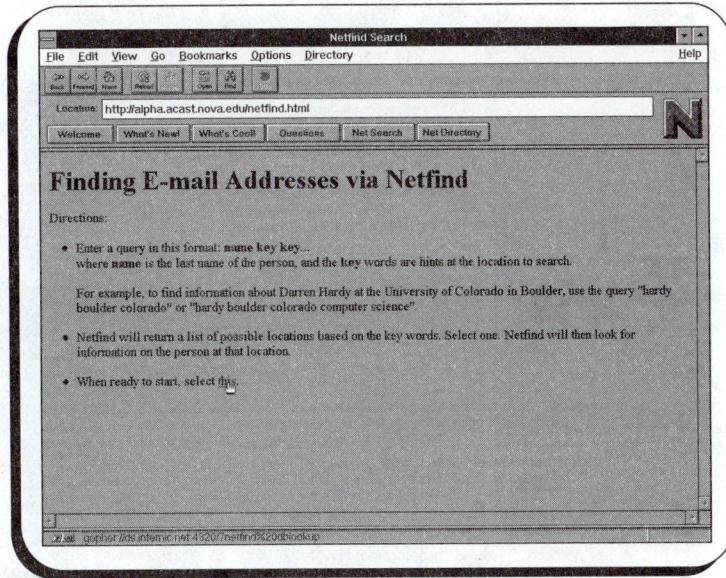

3. In the search screen you see in Figure 8.19, type margolis public health north carolina in the Enter search keywords: field and press Enter. The first word is the last name of the person being searched for and the remaining words are called **keys**. Netfind will produce a list of possible locations where the information might be found given the keys you specified (see Figure 8.20).

FIGURE 8.19
The form for entering the name and the keys to search for a name.

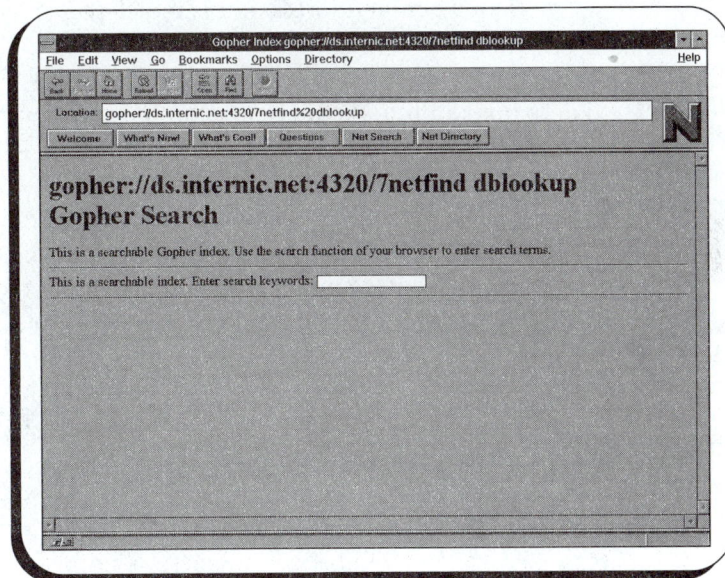

FIGURE 8.20

The results of a
Netfind search.

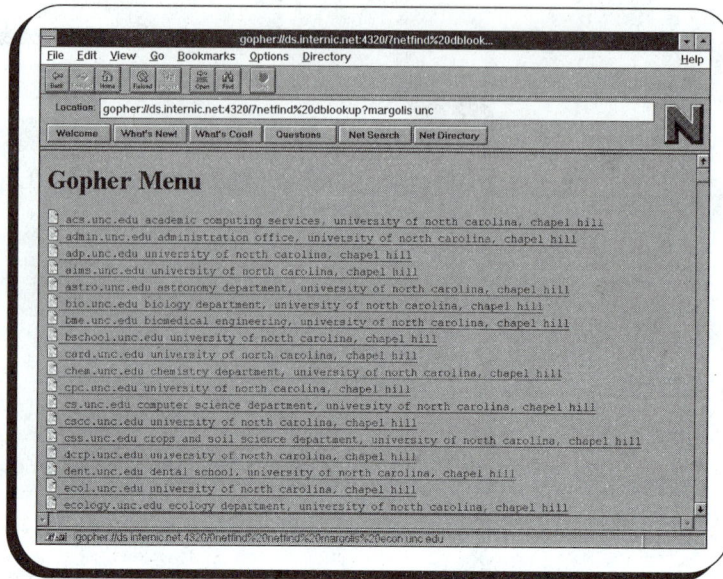

4. Click Edit, and then click Find. You are going to try and find information using the key words in the list you see in Figure 8.20.

5. Click View, and then click Find.

6. Type public in the Find: field. The list entry sph.unc.edu school of public health, university of north carolina, chapel hill, north carolina is found. That's probably where Lew Margolis address is. Click on that entry and Lew's e-mail address, if it is registered, may show up.

FINDING EVERYTHING ABOUT ANYTHING

We're not kidding. As the Net becomes more sophisticated and better indexed, information becomes more readily available. All you need is a good tool to search for that information and that's where the search engines come into play. Table 8.5 displays a listing of all the different search utilities you can use to find information. Some utilities search for the titles of articles according to the name you enter, some for content, and some for both. It would take at least 100 pages to show you how each one works, but keep the following points in mind:

TABLE 8.5   Search tools for the Net.

URL	Name
http://info.cern.ch/hypertext/DaatSources/bySubject/Overview.html	WWW Virtual Library
http://www.einet.net	EINet Galaxy
http://white.mosc.mil/info_modern.html	Planet Earth
http://akebono.stanford.edu/yahoo	Yahoo
http://nearnet.gnn.com/wic/newrescat.toc.html	Whole Internet Catalog
http://www.stir.ac.uk/jsbin/jsii	Jumpstation II
http://www.biotech.washington.edu/WebCrawler/Hone.html	Webcrawler
http://lycos.cs.cmu.edu	Lycos
http://www.cs.colorado.edu/home/mcbryan/WWWW.html	World-Wide Web Worm
http://rbse.jsc.nasa.gov/eiichmann/urlsearch.html	RBSE

1. Each utility allows you to enter terms for which you want to search.
2. Some allow you to use Boolean operators such as AND (e.g., Superman *and* comics) and OR (e.g., Comics *or* Superman).
3. All will return lots of stuff, some relevant to your needs and some not. The more definitive your search terms, the more precise your results.
4. All search utilities are busy. Try and work during off-hours and your results will be returned more quickly.

So point your browser (such as Netscape) to the http address and search! There are a ton of different places where you can seek out information and they start with the various Internet search options available on the Directory menu in Netscape. It might take some experimentation but, in a short while, you will become adept at locating the information you are seeking. Be sure to keep in mind that you can search not only for information about people but also about just any subject. Be brave—and get on the Internet and see what you can find. Good luck!

UTILITY NETIQUETTE You're probably a very polite Internet member by now, but there are a few more things to remember about being a responsible user of the utilities we covered in this chapter. Take a look at Box 8.1 to see what these are.

BOX 8.1
Utility Netiquette

1. Do searches such as Archie during the evening or nighttime hours.

2. Go to the nearest search sites to minimize the distance that a file needs to be transferred.

3. Don't give out e-mail addresses without the permission of the person who owns the address.

4. Utilities such as the Web are new and experimental. When you find a bug or have a suggestion to improve the way one operates, e-mail the developers and share your ideas. You can usually find their e-mail addresses on one of the interface screens.

In this chapter of Hands-On Internet for Windows, we took you on a tour of different utilities you can use to browse the Internet and find information. While this can be great fun, and time-consuming beyond imagination, you will need to practice before you can pinpoint what you want and where to find it. To shorten this time, use the Net as much as possible and listen to your friends and colleagues who might unintentionally come upon some important and useful resources. If you're so lucky, make a note of what you learn so you can share your good fortune.

KEY WORDS

Archie
gopher
gopher client
gopher server
gopherspace
key

SWAIS or Simple Wide Area Information Server
Veronica or Very Easy Rodent-Oriented Net-
    Wide Index to Computerized Archives
WAIS or Wide Area Information Server
WHOIS
World Wide Web or WWW

REVIEW QUESTIONS

1. What is the difference between gopher and Archie?

2. What are some of the types of information you can search for using gophers? Use any gopher site you want and search for one screen of information in an area of interest to you.

3. What are some of the options open to you when you search using ArchiePlex-Forms? When would you use these options?

4. What is the most practical way to find out if your friend has an e-mail address and what it might be?

5. You know that your friend, named Jack Jordan, is at a university with the following domain name: @mnu.edu. Using Netfind, what type of information might you search for?

EXPLORATION EXERCISES

1. Go to any gopher site and list five of the libraries that are available through that site. See if you can find the author of *Gone with the Wind*.

2. Use one of the Internet search engines on the Directory menu of Netscape and search for information on the Apollo moon landing. Note where you found the information and compare notes with your classmates. How many different sites were consulted?

3. Find the Internet Hunt. What is the third question for April of 1993? (*Hint:* gopher to consultant.micro.umn.edu and go to Gopher and Other Information Servers, go to All the Gophers in the World, go to the CICNET gopher server, select Internet Hunt, then find the questions and the answers for April of 1993.)

4. Working with at least two other classmates, find this month's Internet Hunt and try to find the answers.

5. Use ArchiePlex and find five locations for the file `inet.services.txt`, the Scott Yanoff Internet list.

Resources on the Internet

Several times throughout *Hands-On Internet for Windows*, we told you that the Internet has more information than any one person can possibly know about. Fortunately, there are some people so devoted to the Net that they spend a great deal of their time trying to find the best accumulations of such information, such as a list of mail server lists or ftp sites. For example, there's Scott Yanoff's Internet Resources list. Although there are redundancies in these lists, many resources are so valuable that the people who put them together want to make sure that none are missed.

Here is the information you need to find other information. We are also including the sites you can ftp to so that you can get the software that was used for illustrative purposes in this book. Exploring these is great fun—exactly what the Internet is all about.

What you get . . .	*How you get it . . .*
Set of regularly asked questions called FAQs or Frequently Asked Questions	1. ftp to rtfm.mit.edu 2. Change to the directory /pub/usenet/alt.internet.services 3. Get the file named /Internet_Services_Frequently_Asked_Questions_ &_Answers_(FAQ)
List of mailing lists	1. ftp to rtfm.mit.edu 2. Get the file named Publicly_Accessible_Mailing_Lists, _Part_1_8 to 8_8

What you get . . .	*How you get it . . .*
List of ftp sites	1. ftp to rtfm.mit.edu
	2. Change to the directory /pub/usenet/news.answer/ftp-list/sitelist
	3. Get the files named part1 through part7. or mget part*.
	1. ftp pilot.njin.net
	2. Change to the directory /pub/ftp-list.
	3. Get ftp.list
List of newsgroups	1. ftp to rtfm.mit.edu
	2. Get the file named List_of_Active _Newsgroups, _Part_I.
	3. Get the file named List_of_Active_Newsgroups, _Part_II. or mget List_of_Active_N*
Lots of FAQs	1. ftp to rtfm.mit.edu
	2. Change to the directory /pub/usenet/news.announce.newusers
	3. Get the file named List_of_Periodic_Informational_Postings,_P{art_1_7. (this is the first of seven parts) or mget the files named Lis t_of_Periodic_Informational*
Scott Yanoff's list of Internet resources	1. ftp to csd4.csd.uwm.edu
	2. Change to the directory named /pub
	3. Get inet.services.txt
List of Internet resources compiled by graduate students at the University of Michigan	1. Go to the World Wide Web
	2. Type g
	3. Type hhtp://http2.sils.umich.edu
	4. Type /~lou/chhome.html and press Enter
Big Dummy's Guide to the Internet	1. ftp to ftp.eff.org
	2. Change to the directory /pub/Eff/papers
	3. Get the file named bdummy.txt
High weirdness (a collection of off-beat resources)	1. ftp to quartz.rutgers.edu
	2. Change to pub/internet/sites
	3. Get the file high.weirdness.by.email
Eudora	1. ftp to ftp.qualcomm.com
	2. Change to quest/windows/eudora/2.1
	3. Get the file eudora (or update)

What you get . . .	*How you get it . . .*
HTML Assistant	1. ftp to ftp.cs.dal.ca
	2. Change to /ntmlasst
	3. Get the file htmlasst.zip
Netscape	1. ftp to ftp.netscape.com
	2. Change to /windows
	3. Get the file n16eiin.exe
NewsXpress	1. ftp to ftp.hk.super.net
	2. change to /pub/winsock-utilities
	3. Get file nx10b3.zip
WS_FTP	1. ftp to ftp.usma.edu
	2. Change to /pub/msdos/ws
	3. Get the file ftp.zip

Getting Out of Trouble

The list of problems and possible solutions that appears below is based on the assumption that your modem and software are installed, set up, and working correctly. In other words, you are able to connect to the Internet connection you are using. This is not such a simple task with some Windows applications and utilties; if you are in a lab, all this should be taken care of for you.

If you are set up properly, most of the problems that you run into are simple and can be solved by you. The others are system problems that you can't fix and you'll know these by the nature of the message you get (such as *Unable to connect* or *Network error*) when you try to perform a certain command. You don't need a techie by your side or a degree in rocket science to continue to explore the Net. If you run into problems, try and follow these steps.

1. See if you can identify the problem in the column labeled "The Problem." If you can, try the corresponding solution. Be especially careful about typing correctly. It's very easy to make the same typing mistake twice (which is why you made it in the first place!).

2. If you can't solve the problem right off, redo what you have done to see if you can duplicate the problem. Perhaps you'll perform a set-up the correct way this time and solve your problem.

3. If you are still stuck, don't let yourself get frustrated and angry. Stop working, sign off, and come back later to try again. When we get frustrated, we get tired, and then we all make stupid mistakes.

4. Lastly, ask one of your classmates, your instructor, the laboratory manager, or the system administrator for assistance. Be as clear as possible as to the nature of the problem and why you are not able to complete the task at hand.

In some cases, none of the above people will be able to help you since you will be dealing with an Internet resource such as the Web or some database you accessed through WAIS. In that case, try and find the e-mail address for the people who administer the site you went to in order to access these utilities. Then, e-mail them and ask for help.

We learn best by doing. If you solve a problem by yourself, next time you will know how to get around a particular kink in the system. You will also realize that learning will generalize to other settings where you can apply your knowledge to solving other types of problems. Always consult yourself first. You'll be amazed at how smart you are and how much you know about the Internet.

The Problem	*Check This*
ftp Problems	
You can't download a file.	If you have to enter a name, be sure that you are typing file and directory names exactly as they appear with great care given to upper- and lowercase characters.
You don't know what directory or subdirectory you are in.	Use the appropriate commands to move up and down the directory to see where you are. Most ftp utilities also show what directory you are in.
You downloaded a binary file but it does not work.	You have to indicate binary file before the download process begins.
You can't connect.	Some anonymous sites limit their hours. Read what the limits are (they'll tell you) and try to connect during the specified hours.
A file you downloaded can't be read or doesn't work as it is supposed to.	The file may be compressed. Check the file extension (such as .zip or .arc) and the correct utility to uncompress the file before trying to use it.
General Problems	
Can't connect to a gopher server.	Try again in the late evening or early morning when the sites may not be fully busy.
Don't know your e-mail address.	Call your system administrator or have someone who knows your address send you mail. Then, look to see what your address is. Or, you can subscribe to a list and look for the address that it uses to mail back to you.

The Problem	Check This
It worked yesterday but does not work today.	Try to remember if you changed anything including settings on your computer, operating system adjustments, addition of hardware. Computers are constructed so that the slightest change in one element can affect the performance of another, even though you may think they are entirely unrelated.
Nothing is happening on the monitor screen.	Sometimes the Internet is very busy. Wait five minutes before you try to reconnect.
The commands you enter or buttons you click don't get the desired response.	Be sure that you are entering characters in the exact required upper- or lowercase. This is especially important when you are working with files.
You need help.	Look for a Help menu or a Help option.
What you see on your monitor screen is not the same as what you see in this book's illustrations.	The Internet is constantly changing. Try to mimic the general procedures and not be too concerned about correctness.
You want a general introduction to some component of the Internet.	Search for FAQs (frequently asked questions) about the topic.
You can't connect to an anonymous ftp site.	You provided your mail address rather than the word anonymous, or vice versa.
You can't connect to an Internet host.	Be sure that you have spelled the address of the host correctly.
You need to cancel an operation.	Try the Ctrl-C or Ctrl-X key combinations.
You see every character that you typed.	In your communications package, turn Echo off.
You can't connect to an Internet address.	Try the IP number. You may have copied the address wrong. And if you use the number to connect and can't, try the FQDN for the same reason.
You get an Unknown Host message back and can't connect.	Be sure that you typed the address correctly. If this does not work, wait 15 minutes and try again. The host may be busy.
You can't see what you typed on the monitor screen.	In your communications package, turn Echo on.
You can't connect.	The connection might be off-line or no longer functioning. Try again later.
You forgot your password.	Call the system administrator and explain the problem. Be ready to provide a new password if such is needed.

The Problem	Check This
Your attempted connection is timed out.	It took too long to make the connect to the Internet computer. Disconnect and try again.

Mail Problems

The backspace key does not work to delete characters.	Use the delete key.
You don't see mail that you sent yourself right away.	Be patient. It sometimes can take hours for mail to get from one address to another.
You get a Host Unknown message back when you try to send mail.	You either entered the e-mail address incorrectly or you entered an incorrect address. Try the address you have and if that does not work, try to contact the person to verify the e-mail address.

News Problems

Been vacationing and have too much to read?	Select the catch-up option which will mark all unread news as automatically read.
You subscribed to a mailing list and your mailbox is full.	Check your messages every day or unsubscribe to the list.
You are having trouble unsubscribing to a mailing list.	Be sure that the only thing in your message to the list server is Unsubscribe or Signoff.
Your signature gets cut off at three lines.	Some systems limit signatures to three lines.

Telnet Problems

You can't connect to a certain site.	Not all telnet sites are anonymous. Contact the postmaster and ask him if you can get a temporary account number.
You entered the correct telnet address, but didn't get the result you expected.	You forgot to include the port after the address.
You are trying to connect to WWW at CERN in Switzerland and it's taking a long time.	This connection across the world is often slow to be realized. Connect to a closer server.

Answers to Review Questions and Exploration Exercises

CHAPTER 1   Review Questions

1. The federal government initially supported research and military networks, from which the Internet descended. Currently, the federal and state governments support institutions that are connected to the Net.

2. The Internet is managed by supervisors or system administrators at each Internet site. It is paid for by everything from tuition to special fees to customer fees, if a private connection is being used. The best way to ensure that the Internet stays healthy is for those people who use it to attend to, and follow, the informal rules and standards that have been developed.

3. Being verbally abusive, flaming at someone because you don't like him or her, and playing some game against someone in Finland for four hours are all activities that are not looked upon kindly by the majority of Internet users.

4. Talk to other students as well as colleagues to get the information you need to answer this question.

5. Compare the answers you get from one faculty member to another and see if there is any consensus.

Exploration Exercises

1. Share these questions with a classmate. Later on, go back to these questions and see which might be the "easiest" or most "difficult" to answer.

2. There is a ton of stuff on the Internet in the popular literature and almost every popular magazine has something. Share the summaries with a classmate.

CHAPTER 2 Review Questions

1. Almost nothing! Just a connection to the mainframe computer.

2. Advantages are that they usually offer incentives for signing up, have front-end software, and have help available on-line. The big disadvantages are that they can be expensive and do not offer all the Internet utilities and options.

3. An IP address is expressed as numbers (such as 129.237.34.1) and domain names are expressed in names and characters such as falcon.cc.unkans.edu.

4. neil is too easy to guess and could be changed to leni. abcdef is too easy to guess since the characters are a sequence could be changed to aabbcc. Internet is too obvious and could be changed to InTeRnEt or iNtErNeT.

5. While all of these may be present, not all are essential: the name of the computer connection, subdomain representing where the computer is housed, the institution where the computer is housed, and the type of site.

6. The system administrator is usually responsible for assigning account numbers and tries to do so in such a way such that no two people have the same account and so that the account reflects the owner (such as ns for Neil Salkind).

Exploration Exercises

1. Ask a consultant at your computer center or your instructor if you need help.

2. Compare the ten you come up with those your classmates discover.

3. After you have read the material you receive, which of the services would you try?

4. Keep in mind that you have to adhere to system requirements and make sure that everyone has his or her own unique account.

CHAPTER 3 Review Questions

1. The WWW is a collection of protocols or rules that guide how information is presented and transferred from one Internet site to another.

2. Among the five, you might find the following: ease of transferring files, ease of jumping from one document to another, sending mail, finding information, sharing your own information.

3. A home page is a location on the WWW, and HTML, or hypertext markup language, is the language used to create one.

4. HTTP stands for hypertext transfer protocol, the rules of exchanging information on the WWW. HTML is the language used to create home pages.

5. A bookmark marks the URL for a home page, allowing you to return to it quickly and easily.

Exploration Exercises

1. Try to share your enthusiasm for the Net and the WWW with your colleagues and show them a Web page that might touch on some of their interests.

2. All home pages have a URL and many have common elements such as a title, hypertext links, and more. Print them out and try to define the commonalities.

3. Home pages change when the person who designed the page changes it, perhaps to reflect new information or new additions and such. Remember, the Net is a dynamic entity that changes every day or even every hour.

4. Bookmarks help you trace your activity and allow you to go from location to location with a minimum of effort.

5. Look for the release date and the version number of the Help menu.

CHAPTER 4   Review Questions

1. Advantages: easy to use, very quick, and inexpensive. Disadvantages: no privacy, you can't take back what you say once that send button is pushed, and lack of a paper trail.

2. Eudora is menu-driven, allows you to send and accept mail, and is also a fully featured mail application. Netscape only lets you send mail.

3. The In box shows you what mail is new or has been processed. The Out box lists mail that has already been sent.

4. An • represents mail that is new and unread, an R represents mail that has been read and replied to, and a blank space represents mail that has been read but not replied to.

5. Click Help and then locate Save.

Exploration Exercises

1. Eudora enters Harrite plus the home domain name, you send the mail and it never gets there because it was not addressed correctly.

2. The system operator will probably create a file with these answers and send them to anyone who asks these questions.

3. You can copy messages to anyone and everyone using the simple cc: feature.

4. Using nicknames really makes the use of Eudora convenient.

5. Remember that signatures always appear at the end of a message until they are changed.

CHAPTER 5   Review Questions

1. You can use ftp or e-mail. ftp is convenient because with one command you can easily go to another site where you can then explore what's available. Although e-mail is not as convenient, it can be used on almost any system including those that have just the plain mail command.

2. Enter the word *anonymous*. That's how the site recognizes an outside user. It's also how you know the site is open to outside users.

3. ChgDir—changes to another directory. MkDir—makes or creates a new directory. ← loads the selected article to the open directory.

4. The highest level is doctor. The complete directory path is doctor/medical. The file is ASCII format.

5. Select all the files by using the Shift key as you click on the file.

6. A compressed file is one that is reduced in the amount of space it occupies. You can tell a file is compressed if it has an extension such as .zip or .lha. See the table in this chapter that defines such extensions.

Exploration Exercises

1. Mitch Kapor.

2. pub/music/lyrics/folk/s "Coming for to carry me home."

3. Five questions and the editor is Eugene Garfield.

CHAPTER 6   Review Questions

1. The main set has traditionally included those that have been used more often and contain more information.

2. NewsXpress, but there are many other examples.

3. An article is part of a thread, and threads make up a newsgroup.

4. Because USENET is organized as a hierarchy where newsgroups contain threads and threads contain articles.

5. You would unsubscribe if you were no longer interested in a newsgroup. You no longer receive news about the group. You may want to subscribe since the content of the group changes or your interests change.

6. Netscape allows you to read news but NewsXpress provides you with many more options including mailing news and posting articles. The biggest advantage is that NewsXpress allows you to see all the available newsgroups.

7. Along with other files in your Internet connection account.

8. Your mail box may become so full that you can't "pull" anything out of it. None of what you want to read will be accessible.

Exploration Exercises

1. It will surely start with a!

2. There may be many newsgroups you don t have a chance to read. If you find one you really want, ask the system administrator to consider getting it.

3. You can have lots of fun sharing new and exciting information with friends (and yourself!).

CHAPTER 7 Review Questions

1. It's like e-mail in that you can exchange information with other Internet participants. For example, several bulletin boards allow you to send mail and respond to user inquiries.

2. A client is the source of the telnet command. A host is the computer that you are telnetting and connecting to.

3. The remote computer is the one you telnet to and one that you control from a remote location such as the terminal in your lab or your computer at home.

4. The open command opens access to a particular telnet host. The close command closes access to a particular telnet host. These should be used at the telnet > prompt.

5. They can both be used to telnet to another computer, but Netscape uses the telnet application to make the connection indirectly.

Exploration Exercises

1. The response depends upon the time of year.

2. This is fun and free (and possible useless) therapy.

3. 180 minutes.

4. Your answer depends upon the month you telnet to this university of Montana site.

5. About the Book SIG.

CHAPTER 8   Review Questions

1. A gopher is a menu-driven utility that connects you to different Internet resources. Archie is a utility that finds file locations.
2. You can search for information about almost any topic using any of the search tools that were discussed.
3. Where to search, what number of results you want, what you want to search for, and more.
4. Call on the phone or write a note.
5. His e-mail address at mnu.edu.

Exploration Exercises

1. Use the database from the University of Colorado that we illustrated in this chapter.
2. Your classmate can read the review using Eudora or any other mailer.
3. You can find questions for all the Internet Hunts at the location we are describing.
4. These are tough questions, but the exercise is lots of fun. See what you can do!
5. You should see a list of all the people on your connection. You may not be able to find your classmate's address through WHOIS, since not every name is registered.

The Changing Nature of Netscape

We told you this would happen! As we warned you several times, the Internet is a moving target and what's there today won't be there (or at least in the same order) tomorrow. Such is the case with Netscape. Shortly after this book went into production, the Netscape people changed the look of Netscape and added some nice additions which I will discuss here. Everything that you already learned about Netscape certainly still applies. It's questionable whether you might have even noticed the changes.

So here's what's really new with Netscape.

1. The opening Netscape screen, as you can see in Figure D-1, is different. That's the bad news. The good news is that almost all the options on the previous version of Netscape remain, so you can just click away and accomplish the same thing as before.

FIGURE D.1

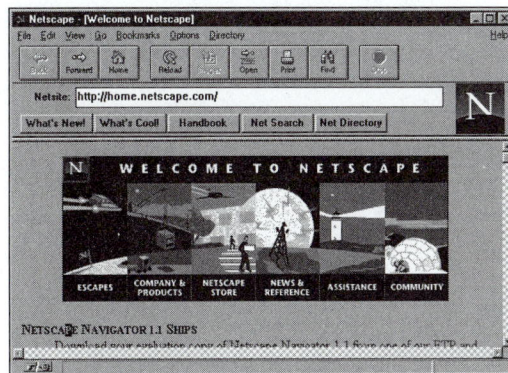

2. You can now right-click (click the right mouse button) when at a URL site and make a bookmark by selecting the appropriate option on the right-click menu (as shown in Figure D-2). You also perform a host of other operations using the right-click method such as go Back or Forward, save an image as a file, and even create a bookmark without having to go to a menu.

FIGURE D.2

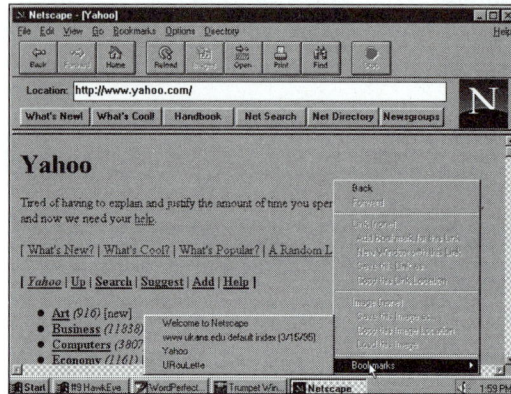

3. And yes, there are all kinds of new links from the opening Netscape page, and you'll have to explore them on your own. One thing you should know is that the ArchiePlex form (see Chapter 8) is no longer available at the Net Search menu, but rather at the following URL:

http://pubweb.nexor.co.uk/public/archie/archieplex/cgi-bin/
archieplex/server=archie.doc.ic.ac.uk

It's a long URL, but worth it. You can also use any of the Netscape search tools and enter ArchiePlex to find other locations.

Index

Why We Go To Zoos